ON DRAG-HUNTING

ON DRAG-HUNTING

JOHN STRAWSON

Delightful scene!
Where all around is joy, men, horses, dogs;
And in each smiling countenance appears
Fresh blooming health.

J. A. ALLEN

The author and publisher are grateful to the following for permission to reproduce the paintings, drawings, sketches and woodcuts referred to:

Paintings and sketches by Snaffles – Felix Rosenstiel's Widow & Son Ltd
Drawings by Sir William Nicholson – Mrs Elizabeth Banks
Paintings by Lionel Edwards – Mr Ken Edwards and Mr A. N. Lyndon-Skeggs
Painting by John King – Mr John King and Mr A.N. Lyndon-Skeggs
Woodcuts by B.B. (Denys Watkins-Pitchford) – David Higham Associates
Paintings and sketches by Gilbert Holiday – Mrs Jane Westcott

The drawings of Sir William Nicholson first appeared as illustrations for Siegfried Sassoon's *Memoirs of a Fox-Hunting Man*, 1954 edition. Denys Watkins-Pitchford's woodcuts illustrated his own book, *Wild Lone: The Story of a Pytchley Fox*, 1970 edition.

Further acknowledgements for the help given to the author and publisher with regard to these illustrations are given in the Acknowledgements on page 9 of this book.

British Library Cataloguing-in Publication Data.
A catalogue record for this book is available from the British Library.

ISBN 0.85131.757.X

Published in Great Britain in 1999 by
J. A. Allen
an imprint of Robert Hale Ltd.
Clerkenwell House,
45-47 Clerkenwell Green,
London, EC1R OHT.

Typeset in Cambridge by Textype Typesetters Ltd.
Printed in Hong Kong by Dah Hua International Printing Press Co
Designed by Judy Linard

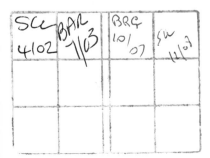

Contents

Illustrations

Acknowledgements

This short book came to be written because of the fortunate circumstance that just as I was hoping to record my experiences of drag-hunting, the publisher, J. A. Allen & Co Ltd, was on the lookout for someone to write a more general book on the subject. It therefore seemed appropriate for these two designs to be combined and I am most grateful to Caroline Burt of J. A. Allen & Co. for her ready agreement to the publication of some of my own recollections of days spent out drag-hunting. I am also specially indebted to Pat Sutton, Chairman of the Masters of Draghounds Association, who had previously embarked on, but had been obliged to discontinue, a similar mission, for her enthusiastic support and for providing me with material which she had collected. Pat Sutton has been joint Master and Huntsman of the Staff College and Royal Military Academy Sandhurst Draghounds for more than twenty years, and her knowledge and experience of the sport are profound, as her introduction to this book so clearly demonstrates. My own time as Master and Huntsman of the Staff College Drag was very much shorter but my enjoyment of it was, I believe, equal to hers.

When Pat Sutton was assembling material for her own purpose, a number of drag hunts provided her with information about their history and activities, which she has kindly placed at my disposal. Since then I have also been able to collect contributions from other packs of draghounds, which furnish much of the material for this book. It has not been possible, however, nor would it be desirable to obtain detailed accounts of *all* such packs, for to have presented a surfeit of drag-hunting stories to the reader would hardly have earned his or her gratitude. It is to

9

be hoped though that what is included will satisfy both those who know something of the sport and those who do not. I have allowed myself the indulgence of including personal anecdotes and of drawing upon literary allusion.

It will be seen from the list of existing packs of draghounds (see page 194) that at present there are sixteen of them in Great Britain and the Channel Islands and one in Ireland, and it is pleasing to observe that they are widely spread throughout the country and include the Isle of Man, Jersey and Anglesey. Those drag hunts which responded to Pat Sutton's request for information were the Berks and Bucks Draghounds, the West Shropshire, the Mid-Surrey Farmers' and Cambridge University Drag Hunt. We are most grateful for these contributions which have been invaluable. Many others have assisted me and I am greatly indebted to all of them. I am particularly grateful to the following: Lieutenant-Colonel Conway Seymour, Regimental Adjutant, Grenadier Guards and Captain David Horn MISM, Curator, The Guards Museum, for allowing me to study *Household Brigade Journals* and for providing me with extracts from these journals; the Household Division for permission to quote from them; Captain Horn for also kindly arranging for copies of two paintings to be made; Captain Damer Colville for letting me examine and quote from the hunting journals, diaries and other papers of the Royal Artillery (Woolwich) Drag and the Royal Artillery (Bordon) Drag – these documents being in his family's care, as his father and uncle were masters of these two packs – and also for providing photographs of the Woolwich Drag; Mr Andrew Lyndon-Skeggs, former Master and senior Trustee of the Cambridge University Drag Hunt, for his generous help in providing information about the CUDH and transparencies of pictures by Lionel Edwards and John King; Mr Ashley Brodin, Joint Master of the Oxford Draghounds, for his ready assistance with information about his Hunt; Brigadier K. A. Timbers, Historical Secretary, Royal Artillery Historical Trust, for his instant response to my questions about Royal Artillery drag-hunting and for supplying me with copies of Gilbert Holiday's paintings and sketches of the Royal Artillery (Woolwich) Drag; Major John Hunter, Headquarters, Director Royal Artillery, for putting me in touch with Brigadier Timbers; Major-General Arthur Denaro CBE, Commandant, The Royal Military Academy Sandhurst, for his invaluable help in alerting his staff to assist me and for providing photographs of the Drag in Co.

Londonderry; Dr P. J. Thwaites MA MSc, DMS, AMA, MIMgt, Curator, Sandhurst Collection, for sending me a brief history of the Staff College Drag and other material; Major Stephen Connelly for helping with my examination of the Staff College archives and for supplying me with papers, pictures, sketches and photographs of the Staff College Drag; Mr David Allardyce, Photographic Section, Joint Services Command and Staff College, for producing transparencies; Mrs Jane Westcott, granddaughter of Gilbert Holiday, for her support and most generous permission to reproduce some of his paintings and sketches; Colonel A. J. Blad, Mrs Westcott's cousin, for further help with Gilbert Holiday's work; Mr William Marler for his invaluable advice about the copyright of Gilbert Holiday's work; Mr Oliver Swann for his most helpful advice about copyright matters generally; Mr Richard Repetto-Wright for his copyright assistance; Colonel Jasper Browell MBE for arranging with the King's Troop to provide a picture of the Royal Artillery Drag; Maura Rutter, *Baily's Hunting Directory*, for her instant, generous help.

I am deeply indebted to the works of B. B. (Denys Watkins-Pitchford), Peter Beckford, Siegfried Sassoon, R. S. Surtees, G. M. Trevelyan and Anthony Trollope. The author and publisher wish to thank *Baily's Hunting Directory* (Pearson Publishing Ltd) for permission to reproduce the section on draghounds from their 1998–99 publication.

The author and publisher are grateful to the following for permission to reproduce pictures and illustrations in this book: Mrs Jane Westcott; Rosenstiel's (Felix Rosenstiel's Widow & Son Limited); Mr Ken Edwards; the Committee, Staff College and RMA Sandhurst Drag; Mr Andrew Lyndon-Skeggs; Mr John King; Major-General Evelyn Webb-Carter OBE and the Household Division; David Higham Associates (on behalf of B. B. – Denys Watkins-Pitchford); The King's Troop, Royal Horse Artillery.

I am grateful to the following for their help in my research concerning the work of Sir William Nicholson: Elizabeth Duggan; the National Art Library; the Publishers' Association; Mr Giles de la Mare. I wish to thank Mrs Elizabeth Banks for her kind permission to reproduce four drawings by Sir William Nicholson, and I would like to add my thanks to Mr Andrew Nicholson and Mr Desmond Banks for their assistance in this matter.

I wish to thank my son-in-law, Tim Barker, for his invaluable help in making transparencies of pictures and photographs, and my daughter,

Carolin, for her research into copyright matters.

In recounting some of my experiences as Master and Huntsman of the Staff College Drag, I have drawn on some stories I wrote for *Blackwood's Magazine* in the 1960s and 1970s. I have also made use of an article called 'Foxhounds to Trieste', which appeared on the Court Page of *The Times* in the early 1960s and was republished in the anthology *Right Hand Court*, The Times Publishing Company Ltd, 1965. I should add that my request to *The Times* for their agreement did not yield a reply.

I would like to thank the photocopying staff of Coates & Parker, Warminster, for their cheerful, courteous and efficient help in making copies of my typescript.

Finally I wish to thank my wife for her invaluable assistance in the preparation and production of this book.

Introduction

When John Strawson asked me to write an introduction to this book, it caused me to stop and ponder on just how much of my life has been involved with drag-hunting. I am a great believer in the old saying: 'What you put in, you get out' and I certainly have had an enormous amount of fun and enjoyment over the years even though at times it has been really hard work.

Those of you who have managed a line for your local drag hunt will know how much time you need to spend on this. The most important person on any day out with a drag pack is the farmer or landowner whose land you are riding over. It is entirely because of their kindness and goodwill that we can enjoy a day in the countryside. Part of the line manager's job is getting out on to the farms and discovering routes so as to maximise the use of grassland and stubble with as many fences as possible.

Those drag hunts which are in countryside with well-kept hedges have a head start, whereas others, on open downland or in heavily wired farmland, require many fences to be built and maintained. The route of each line and the position of every new fence will have been discussed and agreed with the farmer well before the day's drag-hunting. Even then, the

Staff College Hunt staff and hounds 1982/3. Pat Sutton centre, next to Master

13

line manager must be able to cope with a sudden change in the line because of weather or the farmer's altered plans.

It is, of course, essential that the runner is familiar with the exact route. This is usually done by walking the course with the line manager. Similarly the huntsman and field master must know the line perfectly. In general, farmers will allow the huntsman and whips to follow hounds should they lose the scent, but the field should always stick to the agreed route. Members of the field should not assume that a particular line will always be the same. Changes from the previous season will be made. If the field members do go wrong, it will be for the master to go to the farmer with apologies, and this, I can assure you, can be a humbling experience.

The most important requirement for a drag hunt follower is a horse that will jump – an absolute necessity if you wish to enjoy your day. Most genuinely capable horses will cope with average fences; they don't need to jump a house! Your local drag hunt will advise you as to the size and nature of their fences. There is usually a way round a series of larger fences, or alternatively there will be a smaller obstacle or a gateway to ensure you keep up.

I have been most fortunate in having a wonderful succession of good ponies and horses which kept me at the front with hounds. The huntsman's horse, who has, of course, to be in the lead, must be very special. You will see how John Strawson's mare, Bella, was just this when you read about his adventures as master of draghounds. My own first 'special' was a 16 h.h. mare called Nancy. I hunted hounds from her for five seasons and she was a really tough sort who would jump anything to stay with hounds. My second 'special' was Mr Mole, 17 h.h., far too big and strong for me really but we agreed to differ most of the time. I hunted the Oxford Draghounds from him for two seasons when there was no undergraduate to carry the horn. He was the most extravagant jumper of hedges and nothing was too big or too wide. I had some tremendous days across Oxfordshire on him. My last and best 'special' was Bee Gee. He and I hunted the Staff College and Royal Military Academy Sandhurst Draghounds for twelve seasons and he certainly knew how to throw his heart over his fences. He adored hounds and we had many exciting days following them.

I vividly remember my first day out with the Staff College and RMAS Drag. I was about eight years old, the pony was called Fidget and she ran away with me on every leg of the line on Barossa Common. I loved every minute! Over the next few years I spent every spare moment at the hunt kennels and learned an enormous amount from the kennel huntsmen. Firstly, George Collop, who was endlessly patient in teaching me how to whip-in properly to a pack of foxhounds – George making it quite clear with a sharpish tongue when he judged that I was not doing the job 'properly'. Secondly, Michael Jackson and his wife, Molly, who between them kennelled both the Staff College Draghounds and the Sandhurst Beagles. They too taught me a lot.

When I was asked to hunt the drag in 1977, I never thought I would be carrying the horn until 1997. Michael too was incredibly patient and put up with the mistakes I made. Equally long suffering, I'm sure, were the foxhound bitches that I hunted. Between them all I have had some wonderful times and I have been able to store away many exciting memories. Through drag-hunting I have been privileged to meet and make friends with people from all walks of life countrywide.

The sport draws together horsemen and horsewomen who enjoy the challenge of riding across country and jumping natural fences. On some days, packs I have ridden with have been joined by Olympic standard riders, sometimes on their old, famous horses having a jolly, at other times on a younger horse needing to gain experience of cross-country work in all weathers and on all types of going. But many of those following hounds are weekend riders on a Riding Club horse. Whoever they are, all of them have enjoyed themselves both during and after the day's sport.

I have found that the farmers and landowners who have welcomed me into their homes and on to their land have been unfailingly kind and helpful. In spite of the many troubles and difficulties of modern farming, they have always tried to give us a day whenever possible.

For those of you who feel you would like to try drag-hunting, I would say: nothing ventured, nothing gained! If you and your horse enjoy your first day out, then I'm sure you will go on to enjoy many more. You will see that John Strawson has produced some advice for beginners which you will find as an Appendix on page 189.

The British have always had a reputation as bold cross-country riders and you will see, looking back at the history of drag-hunting, that many of the original packs of draghounds were formed by various regiments and by the Universities of Oxford and Cambridge. Military men firmly believed that a soldier's calibre could be judged by how well he rode across country.

Well, if you have no doubts about your nerve and enjoy taking part in a sport which will give you some thrills as well as some spills, read on! This well-written book will give you a genuine taste of drag-hunting, depicting, as it does, some of the 'highs' that you and your horse can achieve, as well as some of the 'lows'. Above all it tells you what fun drag-hunting can be.

PAT SUTTON
Chairman
Masters of Draghounds Association

Foreword

'Orses and dorgs is some men's fancy. They're wittles and drink
to me – lodging, wife, and children – reading, writing, and
'rithmetic – snuff, tobacker, and sleep.'

Charles Dickens, *David Copperfield*

This book does not pretend to be comprehensive, that is to say it does not give a detailed account of all past and present packs of draghounds. Indeed, to do so would be tedious. By being selective, the book seeks rather to give the flavour of drag-hunting, both as it was and is, and in this way will prove, I trust, to be representative. What is more, whereas a mere catalogue of the origins, developments, personalities and activities of selected packs would run the risk of becoming repetitive, I hope that by recourse to anecdote and literary allusion, the narrative has been enlivened.

The nature and flavour of drag-hunting have perhaps never been so briefly and agreeably described than by Charles Armstrong in his chapter on 'Draghounds' (see page 161) which featured in *British*

*Dismounted
without
permission*

Hunting[1]. He explains that draghunts were usually started by Army officers who sought some amusing diversion during what would otherwise have been intolerably irksome winter afternoons, or by such gentlemen engaged in commerce as had not time enough for hunting properly but who relished a cross-country gallop with draghounds. Armstrong goes on to explain that there would be no such thing as drag-hunting were it not for the generosity of sporting farmers who not only make their land both suitable and available, but often throw in a splendid hunt breakfast as well. He next explains how the scent is arranged and that the runner will, having started perhaps an hour before the hounds, trail his bundle of 'smell' from a rope over what needs to be good scent-holding pasture so that the run can begin about 2 p.m. As for the hounds, they are usually drafted from what Armstrong calls 'superior kennels', probably because of some fault like skirting[2]. Such a hound may well become a good draghunter because the combination of a strong scent and a clear line will not allow him to indulge in his habit of skirting. When it comes to the actual business of following the drag, Armstrong's advice is uncompromising: 'You must therefore ride the line with determination, or decline altogether . . . The gallop throughout is a brilliant ride, often over a big country, with hard, unyielding timbers, and yawning brooks, and other formidable obstacles, that tail off the large majority.' Armstrong then lists a number of both military and other packs of draghounds, although there is a notable omission in that he does not mention two of the packs which were earliest established and are still thriving, those of Oxford and Cambridge Universities.[3]

As Anthony Trollope observed, it is a great thing to ride to hounds and an even greater one to be up with them at the finish. I ardently trust that those of you who ride the course of what now follows will similarly persevere to the finish.

[1] *British Hunting* Edited and compiled for *The Sportsman* by Arthur W. Coaten.
[2] Skirter, a hound that is too independent, will not work with the pack, constantly going off by himself. Peter Beckford condemned such a hound, 'I never forgive a professed skirter; where game is plenty, they are always changing.'
[3] Appendix 2, page 165.

Drag-hunting: a Prologue

'a number of horsemen riding furiously after a nasty smell'
Henry Hall Dixon

There is perhaps only one passage in Peter Beckford's great work, *Thoughts on Hunting*, with which all of us would thoroughly disagree, and that is when he maintains that however lively hunting may be in the field, it is dull to write upon. Not only does he give the lie to his own contention, but think of Somerville, think of Surtees, of Trollope, of Sassoon and many others. Indeed we will do more than think of them. We will call them as witnesses.

It is Beckford who reminds us – with much relevance here – that there have always been those for whom hunting is only to be followed because one can ride hard. And then he asks, 'to such as love the riding part only of hunting, would not a trail-scent be more suitable?'. In posing this question, Beckford brings us face to face with the very *raison d'être* of drag-hunting, for there must be few of those following the sport who have done so except for the challenge and thrill of riding across country over some stiffish fences with the added enjoyment of seeing and hearing hounds in full cry and of participating, no matter how imitatively, in one of our great traditional sports. About those few who do more and know more in making drag-hunting possible, there will be more to say later. But before doing so we must also acknowledge that Beckford made another telling point about the origins of drag-hunting when he is discussing the training of young hounds. In Letter VI he observes to his friend: 'you should like to see your young hounds run a trail-scent'. No doubt he would have been glad to see them run over an open down where their action and their speed could have been perceived and judged. Yet even though doing so once or twice might not hurt the hounds, it was not something that Beckford could recommend for it was one thing to 'stoop hounds to a scent' and quite another to use a trail *after* this has been properly done. Beckford's point about using a trail-scent for the purpose of observing hounds' performance, however, was something which merited wide application as the management of hounds developed. But although during such observation those concerned might be mounted on horses, it had nothing to do with riding to hounds running a trail-scent in order to provide fun for the horsemen. For this purpose, the principal object of our treatise, we must turn elsewhere.

Let us for the moment leap a century and a half from Beckford's thoughts of the 1770s to Siegfried Sassoon's recollections of what it was like to find himself, suddenly and unexpectedly, engaged in a drag hunt. Shortly after the start of one season, Sassoon was feeling dissatisfied with the hunting provided by his local pack of hounds, for most of the time semed to have been spent 'pottering round impenetrable woodlands', and the one brief run they had had ended in him being shouted at – 'Keep that bloody horse well out of my way' – for supposedly following too closely over a fence after the perpetrator of this ill-mannered outburst (the very sort we have all come across at one time or another). Sassoon remembered his 'bumptious and bullying manners', his clumsy and mutton-fisted way with a horse, either bellowing at his groom or 'cursing and cropping the frothing five-year old' carrying his 15 stone, which, happily, often ended up head first in a ditch. These disappointments had the effect of making Sassoon go off to have a day with a neighbouring pack. It was there that he revised his view of hunting and derived great confidence and pleasure from the boldness and stamina of his old hunter.

When the Master decided to draw a small spinney near the best bit of vale country there was, Sassoon's companion, who had already confided in him that the Master had something up his sleeve and that they'd had 'one or two *very queer foxes* lately', quickly saw what was up and told Sassoon to stick close to him, adding, 'The old devil's got a drag laid, as sure as mutton.' A shrill halloa was followed by the sight of the huntsman galloping on with his hounds, with Sassoon and his friend well forward, taking fence after fence in fine style, for the old hunter was a bold jumper, and together they covered about 4 miles of excellent country. It ended with the huntsman 'blowing his horn under a park wall while the hounds scrabbled and bayed rather dubiously over a rabbit-hole'. Sassoon's enjoyment of it was enhanced by being one of only a few to finish the run. His faith in hunting had been restored by negotiating a 4-mile point of a drag-line. And as Sassoon's groom commented when he heard the story: 'If it was a drag they must have gone like blazes!' They *did* go like blazes.

It was an assertion echoed by Anthony Trollope's Lord Chiltern who, when discussing a particular run, which someone has described as fast, made it plain that if this was what you were after: 'You might go as fast with a drag.' There is, however, one reservation to be made here, as all of us who have enjoyed it know. You must have a horse that likes jumping. You may have an ordinary day's hunting and never negotiate a single fence. Think of Mr Jorrocks, who was not afraid of 'the pace' so long as there was no leaping. But the whole idea of going out with the drag is that you present your noble quadruped with lots of fences and have the added joy of seeing the hounds streaming across country in front of you and passionately hoping that you will be up with them at the end of the final leg to observe the huntsman throwing hounds the worry and blowing the kill. It is therefore of particular importance, if you elect to indulge in this special form of equestrian endeavour, that you have a horse that you know will jump. How often have we been told of an animal: 'He'll jump anything if he wants to'? Yes, you say to yourself, but will he jump when *I* want him to? This key question was brought very much to the attention of Trollope's Phineas Finn when the aforementioned Lord Chiltern lent him a horse to go out hunting.

Chiltern told Phineas that he was to have one of the best horses in the stables, but 'you must be particular about your spurs', and he went on to say that Dandolo can do anything that might be asked of a horse.

Although he had been known to baulk, you had to let him know that you were on his back and, with the aid of a pair of spurs, 'he'll take you anywhere'. This was not altogether reassuring and when Phineas came face to face with Dandolo, he saw a fine, strong bay, short-backed and legged, with huge quarters and a wicked eye. Dandolo's groom praised his strength and speed, and, in answer to the all-important question as to whether he could jump, assured Phineas that he could – 'no 'orse in my lord's stables can't beat him'.

'But he won't?' asked Phineas. The reply was not altogether comforting, for the groom said it was only sometimes, and you had to stick to him until he did and then he'd go like a shot and be right for the day. Such reassurances tend to put a weight on the mind of the horseman required to hunt the animal!

Of course, there are those who are regular supporters of a hunt, who appear at the meet, modestly mounted, courteous and quiet, who are never boastful or loud, never get in the way of the hounds or offend against the rules of the game, who seem to enjoy their hunting as well as anyone, and yet who never negotiate a fence at all, who know the country and the likely outcome of a draw so well that, by dint of using roads and tracks and open gates, proceed without any likelihood of taking a fearful toss at some horrid double oxer. What is more – to the almost heartbreaking chagrin of those who have loyally ridden a straight line and boldly tackled every obstacle in sight – these 'skirters' always contrive to be up with the hounds at the end of a run! But in the case of drag-hunting there can be no such distinction. If you're going out hunting with a pack of draghounds, jumping fences is not an option. It is an obligation. All the more reason for having a horse who loves the sport as much as you do.

Mr Jorrocks maintained that horses love hounds and he loved both. Not so Trollope's Mr Harkaway MFH. For him the hounds were everything. They were his hobby and they were perfect. He had been master of these hounds for more than 40 years and as such had given a good deal of satisfaction to the county in general. Social delights he eschewed. He never read a book unless it referred to some veterinary matter. He had no wife or children. All his time was devoted to his hounds. 'To his stables he never went, looking on a horse as a necessary adjunct to hunting, expensive, disagreeable, and prone to get you into danger.' Compliments about his horses left him cold. Kind words about his hounds he received with much pleasure. It was the hounds who did all the work, which horses and men could but observe. While we of today may perhaps agree with Mr Harkaway's care and concern for his hounds, which we as drag-hunting men and women will certainly share, we know too that unless we choose and school and ride our horses with even greater care and concern, we will see little of the hounds when they are hunting a drag-line. Meanwhile, let us get a taste of the sport as it was conducted more than a hundred years ago – at Murrell Green on 14 February 1888:

On Tuesday afternoon Mr H Paul's drag-hounds met at Murrell Green, by invitation of Mr Kennard[1] and Mr Illingworth. The weather was anything but pleasant, and no doubt kept away many who would otherwise have been present. As it was, the snow had all but gone in the neighbourhood of the course by the afternoon though on the higher and more exposed land round about, it was still lying thick. The course, which ran across the farms of Messrs. Steet and Hankin, who kindly gave their permission, was about six miles long, starting at West Green and going by Borough Court, the Crooked Billet, across the road, and then through the meadows to the subway under the railway, where there was a check, the drag being laid on again on the other side of the line. From here the line led over Pot Bridge Farm, by Totter's Bridge, at the back of Trimmer's farm, and Mr Hankin's house at Murrell Green, into the road, finishing at Mr Kennard's house. There were some big fences and awkward places to negotiate, but no serious tumbles resulted. A start was made at 3.30 pm, the field consisting of Mr E Paul, Mr and Mrs Illingworth, Rev. A G and Miss Barker, and Captain Bayford. Mr Paul's horse went lame soon after starting, but a spare one of Mr Illingworth's soon enabled him to get to the front again. Captain Bayford took his fences in capital style, though an insecurely fastened gate fetched both man and horse over a tremendous purler, for which, however, neither seemed much the worse. Miss Barker, mounted on a good fencer, was well to the front, and more than once showed the gentlemen the way, notably over a bit of water and hedge leading from the road into the water meadow just below the Crooked Billet. After a rattling gallop the whole finished in fairly close order, well satisfied with the fun. Captain Bayford and Mr Paul were in the van, the Rev. A G Barker and his daughter next, and after

---

[1] No relation, as far as I know, to the celebrated Lt-Col. Sir George (Loopy) Kennard who hunted the 4th Hussars' pack of hounds in Italy and Germany, of which more later.

them Mr and Mrs Illingworth. We hope that Mr Kennard will be favoured with better weather for his next drag which we understand is likely to come off within a week or two.

There is much of interest to note in this report, some of it showing that little has changed in a hundred years or so. All of us who have been concerned with organising and conducting a day's drag-hunting will remember how much we always owed the farmers over whose land we galloped. We have all seen gallant military men come to grief over tricky fences and, none daunted, remount and overtake the field once more. Many of us have admired the dash and skill of young ladies on pulling horses and been grateful for them giving us a lead over an uninviting water obstacle. And 6 miles was often the length of a drag-line in my day, although we would be more likely to have two checks, rather than one. These considerations are familiar. But a field of only six seems unusually small, and it would have been good to know who ran with the 'smell' – indeed what it consisted of – and whether Mr Paul hunted hounds himself or had a huntsman. Mr Kennard seems to have been one of the landowners involved, but not himself following hounds. We may note too that 3.30 p.m. is late in the day for starting, given a wintry February, although, as those of us who have done it know well, once you get going with a drag, it's not long before the day's over and you are either hacking back to kennels or, if the meet is far from home, getting the horses boxed and the hounds in the van.

Little is said in the report about all the preliminary work necessary before the draghounds meet at all – reconnaissance for a suitable course, or line as we now call it; selection of the places where fences are to be negotiated, and marking them, although, of course, in 1888, with more natural fences and little or no barbed wire[2], the options of where to jump an obstacle would have been far more numerous; showing the line-layer where to start the drag, the course itself, where to check and lay on again, where to finish; whom to invite to the meet and how to tell them (nowadays easily done by sending a notice of future meets to all hunt members); arrangements for the opening, and subsequent closing, of gates

---

[2] Although farmers who objected to having their fields rampaged over and rails and fences smashed, began in the 1870s to use wire, even barbed wire, as fencing.

if necessary, and the repair of damage to fences. But such details of organisation could not be expected to feature in an account of the drag itself and the fun it provided for those taking part. Nor do we hear how many couple of hounds Mr Paul had, or whether the kennels and his own stables were near to the Kennard or Illingworth houses and so within hacking distance of the meet, but these matters again would be familiar to all those interested and living near Murrell Green. What we can safely say is that the day was a success and that no one appeared to have caused any annoyance by breaking what Mr Harkaway would have called the laws of drag-hunting.

Alas, the same could not be said of a day shortly after the Second World War when I was on leave from my regiment, stationed in Italy, where we, the 4th Hussars, had our own pack of draghounds. I had been out with them and despite coming to grief from time to time by dismounting without permission, in other words taking a crashing fall, while negotiating some formidable stone walls in the Basovizia country near Trieste, I had not disgraced myself. I therefore accepted an invitation for a day with a pack of draghounds in England during my leave. When I arrived to stay with a farmer friend who was going to let me ride his reliable old hunter, Bounty, he told me that the mare was lame, but that the Master's wife, knowing I had but a few days' leave and anxious that I should not be disappointed, had generously offered to mount me on one of her point-to-pointing animals. His name was Pacifico, and as I discovered when I joined him at the meet, never was a gelding more ill-named. Rather like Mr Sponge's Multum in Parvo, there was nothing which on first appearance gave any indication of the mischief and vice of which he was capable. While standing near the village green after coming out of his box, he seemed to have a steadiness and dignity wholly in keeping with the office of his owner's husband. Perhaps he was one of those geldings who prefer to be ridden by a female of the species, for no sooner had I positioned myself in the saddle and begun to adjust my leathers than he started behaving like the member of a circus. Rearing, cavorting, all four legs off the ground at the same time, it was a wonder I stayed on board, and we became the centre of disapproving attention. I overheard phrases like: 'The cavalry isn't what it used to be'; 'No control at all, you know', and 'Which regiment did you say he was in?' I saw the force of Mr Jorrocks's comment that 'there was no young man wot would

Snaffles

Mr Jorrocks finds fault with a member of the field

not rather have a himputation on his morality than on his 'ossmanship'. It was all very humiliating and I was horribly conscious of letting down my farmer friend. Had this been all there was to it, however, I would have been a happy man.

There are some horses who are the very essence of proper conduct under all circumstances except one – when they hear the hunting horn. *Then* they turn into uncontrollable beasts, determined to be at the front of whatever equestrian cavalcade may be taking part in the affair, totally indifferent as to whether they discard their rider or allow him to join in the fun, utterly unconcerned about the severity of any obstacles placed between them and their goal, and with an irresistible desire, which will brook no curb, to be in at the finish. Now, in the drag-hunting field this is all very well, indeed almost a virtue, provided you are well clear of others – in short if you are hunting hounds yourself and absolutely required to be in the lead. By taking Pacifico well away from the other horses at the meet, I had temporarily reasserted some sort of stability, and did not yet know that, to his vices, Pacifico added this virtue.

As the huntsman blew the customary short note on the horn for moving off, all restraint was removed. Pacifico proceeded to display even more affinity to Multum in Parvo, who, it will be recalled, would not only carry his rider into the midst of hounds at a meet, but would think nothing of

26

upsetting the master himself in the middle of the pack. Pacifico was quite up to both these tricks and I was invited to 'move' off. I did so, but not, alas, out of trouble. Pacifico, having been restrained and fallen back a little from those riding behind the Master, hounds and whips, suddenly gave a great plunge forward, almost unseating me, and now, with a thundering of hooves, showers of sparks coming up from the road as his shoes encountered it, was literally charging towards the hounds. Scattering those in the way, he then absolutely *leapt* over them. Terrible oaths from Master and huntsman burned my ears as I set off in a John Gilpin-like manner for heaven knew where! At least we had not ridden over hounds. We had jumped them!

It took me the best part of a mile to get Pacifico under any sort of control. We were galloping wildly along a country road, sometimes on the verge, sometimes on the fortunately rather rough surface, and I was dreading that we should either come to a crossroads or meet some vehicle coming the other way. I had no expectation of anything, short of a racing car, catching us up from behind. But how was I to stop him? 'Diseases desperate grown', Claudius, King of Denmark, tells us, 'by desperate appliances are relieved, Or not at all.' Quite so! It was with desperation that I applied my hands and wrists, with all the strength they could muster, to the reins. The trouble was that by this time most of their strength had been exhausted by my previous struggles with the brute. At length, by hooking the reins over my right arm to the elbow joint, standing up in the stirrups and heaving backwards, I managed to slow him down and turn him round. Yet Pacifico still showed no sign of living up to his name. His blood was up after all this excitement; he was quivering, nostrils aflare, ears pricking, dancing about. There was only one thing for it. I rode him into a ploughed field and, sticking near to the headland, attempted that well-known technique of galloping the fidgets out of him. Little did I know Pacifico. He had a mouth like a bull, the strength of ten, and a determination to keep going that made me regard the Master's wife, who had, it seemed, actually ridden him in point-to-points, with real respect. Anyway, I thought, perhaps he would behave a little better now.

I was in luck to the extent that as I retraced our course – this time with more restraint than John Gilpin – I could see that the hounds were just being laid on at the start of the first leg and that the line sloped up a gentle rise toward a copse with several solid-looking post-and-rail fences to be negotiated. The huntsman, Daniel, was well up with the hounds, Master and whips deployed behind him, and the field firmly under the hand of the Field Master, who sternly ordered me to join them. We all had that familiar feeling, half-way between elation at the prospect of a run and apprehension as to our own performance in it.

The Field Master turned his horse slightly and made towards a wide post-and-rail fence about 200 yards away, which led into a grass field where the hunt servants were already galloping and which led to more fences. Keeping Pacifico well clear of the others, I began my approach to the first fence. It was then that I was able to appreciate why Pacifico was such a good point-to-pointer. He accelerated so alarmingly that not only did we jump the post-and-rails level with the Field Master, but because we attacked it from a different angle, we brushed quite sharply against his animal. A great crashing noise, followed by a roar of rage and abuse, pursued us as Pacifico started to close the gap between ourselves and the hunt servants. A quick look back revealed the Field Master on his feet, shaking his fist and still bellowing, while his large grey gelding, entering into the spirit of the thing, was striding on after us.

I took comfort from the thought that I would be off to Dover early next morning to catch a boat to Calais and then on by military train to rejoin my regiment in Italy. But before this more pressing matters had to be attended to. Pacifico had settled to a fast pulling pace, with myself just holding on, for there was little strength left in my wrists to check him. Up to and past the whippers-in we went until I drew level with the Master himself. He shot me a look which combined disbelief with the most furious dislike that I remember ever seeing on a fellow human's countenance. 'Hold hard, you bloody man,' he snarled. The porter in *Macbeth*, you will recall, bewailed the effect of drink on lechery – as provoking the desire, but taking away the performance. Now, even though the effect of the stirrup cup we had all enjoyed at the meet was long since dissipated, my plight was comparable. My desire to hold hard was intense, for my own well-being, let alone the conventions of the drag-hunting field, but as for performance there was none. So it went on. With the futile execrations of the Master pursuing me, Pacifico, who was jumping superbly, soon left him behind, and we were absolutely on the point of overtaking Daniel, the huntsman, on his nearside, when he gave me what was at least a sensible piece of advice.

'Head him towards Sewell's Brook, sir,' he shouted, pointing with whip down the hill and away from the line he was riding. Although my preference would have been to continue riding Pacifico *up*hill in order further to tax his staying power, there was nothing for it but to obey. Transferring my right hand to the left rein, I hauled. Round we came and at a breathless, terrifying pace galloped down the slope towards what I could now see was a broadish brook with a nasty-looking hedge about 30 yards beyond its far bank. Daniel's reasoning was clear – surely that would either stop him or get him out of the saddle – and it did not appeal to me. Yet such was our momentum, together with Pacifico's boldness and skill, for he steadied himself before the brook, that he cleared the water like a bird and went on to soar over the hedge into plough on the other side, mercifully uphill again. I must say my heart warmed to him then. How well I could now understand and endorse Mr Jorrocks's creed about hunting being 'the sport of kings, the image of war without its guilt, and only five-and-twenty per cent of its danger'[3].

I now had Pacifico more under control and, looking up, I could see the hounds, with Daniel and the Master well up, followed by the whips and field, coming round in a great left-handed sweep towards me. They were still about half a mile distant and this gave me time to put into practice Falstaff's recommendation that the better part of valour is discretion. If I stayed in the field, there would be no end to the catalogue of my misdemeanors. I had created havoc at the meet, put the hounds into danger, been run away with, knocked the Field Master off his horse and overtaken the Master himself. I did not wish to be told, as Gerard Maule was by Lord Chilton in *Phineas Redux*, that directly I showed myself in a run, the sport is all over and hounds ought to be taken home. Fortunately I was able to find my way back to where the meet had been. I helped the groom to unsaddle and rug Pacifico, and drove back to my friend's farmhouse. After I had explained what had happened, we agreed that I had better make myself scarce. After all, should either the Master or the Field

---

[3] Here Surtees has borrowed from William Somerville (1675–1742) whose wonderful poem 'The Chase' contains these lines:

My hoarse-sounding horn
Invites thee to the chase, the sport of kings;
Image of war, without its guilt.

Master choose to put in an appearance later in the day, I might discover that the danger of hunting, as compared to war, was far higher than Jorrocks's estimate of five-and-twenty per cent.

All this happened, of course, long before I became responsible myself for the organisation and conduct of drag-hunting, and indeed you might well ask at this point – what are my credentials for writing about the sport? I trust that what follows will go some way to establish my eligibility to do so.

1

Horse and Hound

'The 'oss loves the 'ound, and I loves both.'

Jorrocks

It was with some hesitation and misgiving that I undertook to vary my military career by becoming master and huntsman of a pack of draghounds. I had to ask myself whether I was up to the job. My horsemanship was adequate if not distinguished and I had enjoyed whipping-in in a wholly amateurish fashion to the pack of hounds which the regiment had established in Italy and later Germany. Moreover I was assured that being master and huntsman of the drag demanded no technical knowledge – just a clear head, a fit frame and a stout heart. Nevertheless, I felt obliged to examine my qualifications and inclinations more closely.

A master of hounds, Trollope has told us, must be 'strong in health, strong in heart, strong in purpose and strong in purse' – a recipe not dissimilar to the assurance I had received. The first I was fortunate enough to be; the last I emphatically was not, but happily the Hunt was prepared to help in this respect. Decision therefore resolved itself into whether I could persuade myself that I possessed strength of purpose and heart. As a soldier I could hardly judge myself to be deficient in either. And then I began to convince myself that some of the other qualities which Trollope prescribed as being essential to the make-up of a master of hounds were exactly those which I could boast. 'He must be self-sacrificing, diligent, eager and watchful' – quite! 'He should exercise unflinching authority' – just so! He should be a man 'capable of intense cruelty . . . savage and yet good humoured; severe and yet forbearing . . . he must condescend to no explanation and yet must impress men with an assurance that his decisions will certainly be right' – precisely! Here was the stuff of which generals are made. If such a nonpareil were required to be a master of hounds, was it not possible that, by assuming the mantle, some of these marks would rub off on me? Anyway, it was worth a try.

Yet however much I might convince myself that in regard to character I was just the man for the job, it was clear that there were still a few things I was short of. A hunting cap and a horn could be bought easily enough; knowledge of hounds and how to control them would no doubt be more gradually acquired. But the most pressing of my deficiencies was simply that I had no horse. And although the very nature of a drag has shown us that you can hunt without a fox, it is certain that you cannot hunt a pack of hounds nor, as some maintain, can you be truly chivalrous, without a horse. It was when I made good this deficiency that I also made my first acquaintance with Bella. We have seen that Mr Harkaway, while conceding the need for a horse in order to hunt, looked upon that animal as costly, unamiable and inclined to get you into trouble. But for me the horse has always been the real joy of following hounds, and Bella reinforced my conviction a thousandfold.

She was a bay mare of nearly 16 h.h., alert, friendly and bold, with a serene and steady look which at once led me to think that we would get on well together. When I asked how old she was, no one could tell me with any certainty. More than ten and less than twenty was the most precise estimate given. But her age did not matter. Her legs were sound, her wind good, her spirit undaunted, and she had that priceless quality which every hunting man seeks in his horses and few find. She never refused. Surtees told us that there is no secret so close as that between a rider and his horse. There are some horses which, as you approach a formidable-looking obstacle, let you into their secret early. 'Just try and get me over this fence' is the message they pass to you. Not Bella. 'Try and stop me getting over it' was her challenge and one which I was impatient to accept. I was, of course, compelled to acknowledge a sensation of being quite out of control at the fences, and had to content myself with being reasonably in control between them.

On the first occasion that I rode her I had an uncomfortable time. It was early February, and since I had just agreed to take over the pack before the end of that season, there was no time to lose in learning the job. I therefore went out with the hounds several times as a member of the field. Bella had already been recommended to me as a likely mount, and it was agreed that I could try her out once or twice. 'She takes quite a hold,' I was informed, 'but jumps like a stag.' What I had not been told was that she had often been used for hunting the hounds and was in no doubt that her rightful place was in front.

For those not familiar with the sport, a word about the form that drag-hunting takes may be welcome. The hounds hunt a scent laid over a prepared course or line of some 6 or 7 miles, with probably two checks.

Bella

The fences are mostly natural ones, but some are specially built, and in order to keep damage to a minimum most of them are fairly narrow so that once the hounds have been launched and the hunt servants have set off after them, members of the field, although nominally controlled by a field master, indulge in something dangerously resembling a point-to-point. The first line that Bella and I completed together had comparatively small fences, which she treated like hurdles, and as I floated past the rest of the field and began to draw level with the Master, he treated me to the same sort of harsh indictment as the last of the Brudenells delivered to Captain White at Balaklava – not unlike my affair with Pacifico. I managed to control her, but finished the line breathless, with aching wrists, wondering what would happen when, as Master myself, I would have the responsibility of being in command not only of Bella, but the hounds, the whips and the field as well.

The second occasion on which I went out, still on probation as it were, produced much more of a test for both of us – big fences, heavy going and a really long gallop. As we soared over some of the trickiest post-and-rails, with ditches on either side, leaving behind us a group of jibbing, refusing horses and their furious, frustrated riders, even though she was still pulling like a train, my respect and affection for Bella knew no bounds. Some horses look magnificent at the meet, but rarely complete the course. Bella was quiet and unobtrusive at the meet, but was always up with hounds at the end.

Not long after this encounter I had to hunt the hounds myself for the first time – it was a special end of season meet for the Pony Club – and Bella and I were both still, so to speak, on trial. I had made my preparations as best I could, seen all the farmers over whose land we would ride, walked the line with those who were going to lay the scent, and, a few days previously, conducted a modest rehearsal with a short line near the kennels to satisfy myself that my performance with the horn would pass muster, and that the hounds would be able to grasp who was the new overseer of their destinies.

On the day Bella went perfectly. Out in front she stopped pulling uncontrollably – except at the fences, that is – and settled down to a good, fast hunting pace, as contented to be the Master's mount as I was to be riding her.

I lost not a moment in coming to terms with the Saddle Club, and Bella was mine. I was never to regret it. She was beautifully behaved in the stable, loved the hounds, refused only once, when there was serious danger of landing on a hound, and, except for a cut knee which put her off the road for a week or two, was never lame. She was, in short, the perfect huntsman's horse and carried me superbly for the whole of the next season. Her only fault, if fault you can call it, was that she had an impish sense of fun which would express itself when something unusual had excited her attention or when she sensed that I was not concentrating sufficiently on the task in hand. Her method of recalling me to my duties was simply to throw me over her head, and then to gaze quizzically down at me. Fortunately, she never did it out hunting – she was far too keen on the whole business for that – but once or twice, on less urgent occasions, I was discomforted before I learned to recognise the symptoms. One of these occasions brought home to me with humiliating literalism that pride can indeed come before a fall.

Hound exercise, although routine, is by no means one of the least pleasing aspects of a master's responsibilities. One morning I took the hounds out with two of my whips to assist me. It was one of those mornings when it was not merely a pleasure to get up early, it was almost a duty. With the agreeable reflection that in this case duty and pleasure were synonymous, I drove to the stables where Bella awaited me, admirably groomed, saddled and accoutred by a trooper of the Household Cavalry, who was devoted to Bella and, during the Christmas break, would take her to his own home. What I did not know when I rose that morning was that there lay in store for me an incident which was to tax alike my sense of dignity and my sense of humour. It was also further to enhance my already considerable respect for the perspicacity of Bella.

For most of the morning exercise things went well. The hounds behaved themselves with just the right coalition of alertness and discipline; Bella was on her toes but answering well to hand and leg; the whips played their part with quiet efficiency. As we jogged along, with the hounds clustered round me, one of them periodically throwing me a look of slavish adoration, I felt a justifiable pride in the superlative control which I seemed to be wielding over my little band of quadrupeds. I congratulated myself too soon. As we rounded the corner of a copse on Barossa Common, only a mile from the kennels, pandemonium broke out. There in front of us was a well-known local character who had, countless years earlier, appointed herself both the champion and guardian of all stray dogs in the area. She was pushing a kind of wooden go-cart made of box planks in which were perched three or four cheerful mongrels and from which innumerable leads allowed another dozen or so assorted strays to roam a little further from her authoritative hand. Camberley Kate[1] was taking her dogs for their regular walk.

This appetising sight was too much for the 30 couple of hounds that I had with me. The discipline to which they had accustomed themselves was no match for their inherent hunting instinct. Giving tongue with a harmony that would have warmed Peter Beckford's heart, they surged forward. Far from being dismayed, however, Camberley Kate's charges seemed to be as eager for a pitched battle as the Dauphin was before Agincourt. At this moment an onlooker, had there been one, would have been treated to the spectacle of two opposing commanders-in-chief vainly endeavouring to restore some semblance of order to a situation that was in danger of deteriorating into one as turbulent as that precipitated by Jack Cade. On the one hand, the mistress of strays, unbowed, had drawn not a sword but a whistle, and was producing from it a series of high-pitched notes which seemed rather to urge her troops to more bellicosity than to quiet them. On the other, I, with an oath entirely appropriate to my new calling, had plunged into the midst of the struggle, whip poised, with the intention of showing, so that there should be no doubt for the future, who was master in fact as well as name. At this critical and seemingly inopportune juncture, my faithful Bella decided to take a hand in the affair. With a buck that would have unseated Murat, she deposited me in the very midst of the mêlée.

Remarkably enough, this involuntary gesture had the very effect for which all previous efforts had been unavailing. The stray dogs rallied round their benefactress, who led them soothingly away, and the hounds lavished their affection upon me with an alacrity that left me in no doubt as to the texture of their tongues. Bella and the whips surveyed the scene with ill-concealed satisfaction. With a brittle grimace I hoisted myself back into the saddle and led my reconcentrated forces back to the kennels. But I had to concede that Bella had saved the day.

---

[1] For Sir Arthur Bryant's enchanting portrait of Camberley Kate, see *The Lion and the Unicorn* (Collins 1969) pages 178–80.

Not all my duties were so adventurous. Soon after taking over as Master I understood why huntsmen, kennelmen and so on are called hunt *servants*. I had entered service myself. My first proper inspection of the kennels convinced me that they would not do. It was not the kennels themselves that had been neglected – for what does Beckford say? – 'Keep your kennel sweet and clean!' – but on three sides of the kennel buildings long, rough grass had been allowed to grow untended. It put me in mind of Hamlet's 'unweeded garden, That grows to seed, things rank and gross in nature Possess it merely'. I mustered a team – one of the whips, two cadets, a girl Pony Club member, the kennel-huntsman and myself – and we launched an attack. It took us two afternoons to clear the overgrown surrounds. Our booty? – old bones, tin cans, broken kettles, rusty bicycles, the remains of an abandoned motor vehicle, boxes, iron bars, bottles (some broken and a hazard to horse and hound), a sodden mattress submerging an iron bedstead, bricks, a pair of Wellington boots, tyres, paper galore and a policeman's helmet. Which cadet, now perhaps accoutred as a field-marshal, I asked myself, had perpetrated this last theft and deposit? The clearing operation was followed by bull-dozing, cleaning, fencing and grass-sowing, and before long the whole kennel area had a clean and workmanlike look, and those members of the Staff College and Military Academy who lived in quarters nearby were as pleased as we were.

All this, of course, took place in the spring after the hunting season was over, when the horses were out to grass and there was time enough for make and mend. But late spring and summer entailed another feature of an amateur master's duties which could hardly be described as one of unalloyed pleasure – hound exercise on foot. Have you ever taken 64 dogs for a walk? Unless you are one of those rarities who really can exercise unflinching authority all the time – authority, moreover, which is instantly recognised by every latent rebel in the canine community – I would not recommend it. When I took over as Master of the Drag there were in the pack 24 couple for hunting proper, and eight couple, whose wildness disqualified them from belonging to the former group, for drag-hunting. I shared the duty of exercising them all six days a week with two others. We were usually assisted by cadets and a number of girls whose lives at that time revolved round stable and kennel. At about half past six on two or three mornings a week, I would arrive at the kennels, don a kennelman's white coat, stuff pieces of bread into the pockets, check that my assistants were present, grasp my whip more firmly, pocket my hunting horn, and give the signal to Jack, the kennel-huntsman, to let them out.

Out they would surge, some coupled (usually the draghounds because of their innate wildness) and would rush at me, mill round me, pleading with eyes, tongues and sterns alike for some of the bread. After a few minutes, when my helpers, the whips, had got round them, off we would trudge, ourselves at a fastish walk, the hounds at a slow jog. If, some 45 minutes later, we returned intact, a morning of exercise without incident – and in only about 50 per cent of the cases was this so – I thanked my lucky stars and, after discussing any problems with Jack, returned to the Staff College and the far simpler business of turning ten captains or majors into potential generals. But on the less happy occasions when the hounds got away to explore the woods and scents of Barossa Common, I would find myself futilely shouting hounds' names, blowing the hunting horn, dispatching my lieutenants here, there and everywhere, and eventually, furious and frustrated, returning to kennels with a few odd hounds whose virtuous glances at me were poor compensation for Jack's unspoken yet detectable reproaches. There was nothing to do but go to work and await Jack's telephone call – perhaps by 10 o'clock that morning, perhaps not until evening – to say that the truants were all safely home. As for those qualities that Trollope had recommended, there was no doubt that on these occasions I became savage and severe, yet my good humour and forbearance were less in evidence. I was diligent and eager enough, but the damned hounds were even more eager to riot and diligent in doing so. About my feeling capable of intense cruelty there were no doubts, but on whom was I to exercise this cruelty? Certainly not on the hounds, although from time to time they felt the rough edge of my tongue or whip.

As I got to know them, however, I became more and more attached to them. There were only eight couple of draghounds, so it was easy enough to learn their names. But to know them all, 32 couple, this took time. There was only one way to do it, I found. First, to know all the names by heart, and then slowly but surely, by the process of elimination, fit hounds to names. Some hounds, of course, were so distinctive in appearance or character that this was simple. But then you would find, say, three bitches all from the same litter, with similar markings, similar characteristics and similar names. It was only when you really knew them that their individuality shone clear. How I remember them! Careful and Cautious, Comely and Comical – whoever had the naming of them had second sight, or maybe they grew up to assume the very qualities which their names implied. Havoc, Hazard and Hotspur – day after day at feeding time I would call them over by their names, under the watchful eye of Jack.

It took me three months to learn all the hounds' names, and by then we had got the horses up and I would take the opportunity to exercise the draghounds by themselves so that they would come to recognise me as *their* master. What a lot they were, outcasts you might say from their customary employment, regarded as redundant by some, yet looked on by me with the same complaisance as Touchstone showed to Audrey. 'Ill-favoured' they might be, but they were 'mine own'; it was my 'poor humour . . . to take that that no man else' would. Grateful and Gravity, Vagabond and Vagrant, Terrible and Trollop, Dangerous and Driver, Welcome and Wasteful, Flyer and Fatal, Miscreant and Mutinous, Handsome and Hideous – would I find rich honesty in such a poor house? I did so and more. Bella, like me, loved them all.

Meet at West Court, Arborfield. The author right, with Michael Festing, whip

Bella had already shown how she liked to play a leading role at hound exercise, but what she really relished was a day's drag-hunting. She would always know which was which. The extra grooming she received, with her mane admirably plaited, the sight of me in proper hunting kit, the hounds coupled for the sometimes long hack to the meet – all these were unmistakable signs that she was in for the real thing. And her unfailing courage, good manners and perseverance were qualities – too often lacking in some of those who rode with us – which so endeared her to me that not to visit her in stable or paddock when she was not being exercised would have been to make the day incomplete. Yet a day with the drag could have its vicissitudes.

At the meet we enjoy the centre of the stage, Bella standing quietly under me, my hand resting lightly on the reins. Surrounded by the hounds, to whom I throw an occasional morsel of biscuit or bread, I sip a stirrup cup and persuade myself that I am monarch of what my limited vision commands. An admiring matron comes up to me and tries to draw my attention to the ravishing prettiness of a Pony Club member, who, the matron claims, is gazing at me with the same raptness that Desdemona lavished upon the Moor. I recall Trollope's recipe that a Master of Hounds should be somewhat feared, should be a man with whom others will not care to argue, and, glancing down at the suddenly restless pack, growl that I have enough bitches to look after already.

The field has at last assembled and it is time to move off. Bella stirs excitedly as I put the horn to my lips and blow an appropriate note. What should then happen is that the hounds quietly jog along behind me, flanked by the whips until we reach the place where the scent is laid, and then, released from my iron discipline, give tongue and get on with their business of hunting the line to the first check. But sometimes, with an enthusiasm misguided but not wholly reprehensible, they anticipate my executive order. So it is on this occasion. They have for some time been standing like greyhounds in the slips, straining upon the start, and now at the sound of my warning toot, before I have announced to them that the game is in fact afoot, they are, to put it briefly, off. With no precise purpose, mind you. Waiters with silver salvers swerve out of their way, hard-faced women clutch Boxers to their bosoms, knowing members of the field sneer at the unsuccessful efforts of a set of amateurs to quell the riot. There is only one thing to

do. I ride quickly to where the line begins and give Bella her head.

Now, surely, all will be well. Drawing my horn again I blow the 'gone away' – in confirmation of what has already taken place, as it were – and hope for the best. Sure enough, my charges appear from all directions, pick up the scent, speak with reinforced confidence and overtake me. I heave a sigh of relief and settle down to assist Bella in negotiating the not inconsiderable fences which lie between us and the end of the first leg. Bella, as always, goes like a dream. The theory is that as I jump into the last field of this leg, just behind the hounds, they, encouraged by the whips, will readily rally round me and patiently wait until it is time to move off to the next part of the line. Imagine my horror when I find that no sooner have I joined them than, with unabated energy, they begin to hunt a heel line; that is, the original one in reverse. After a string of oaths, more recourse to the horn, brutal lashing of the whips with my tongue and

Moving off, Tom Hickman left, Michael Festing right. A few moments later the hounds rioted

41

*Arborfield
Brook*

further delays, the hounds return looking aggravatingly complacent, and order is restored. Only Bella is unmoved by it all.

We move off for the next leg. I tell myself that although when sorrows come, they come not single spies, surely nothing else can go wrong. Little do I know. Half-way along the second leg is a sizeable brook. Bella, with her great virtue of never refusing, has soared over it a dozen times before, and I have no qualms about it. But the unpredictable happens. As we reach it, galloping hard, an idle hound is just struggling out onto the far bank. I am confident we can avoid it. Bella is not, and the sharpest refusal I have ever sustained takes place. The entire field is shortly afterwards rewarded by the sight of a Master who is beginning to wonder whether it is all worth the candle, struggling out of the mud, tight-lipped and unsmiling, to remount and, with dampened ardour, ride to the end of the second leg. The final leg goes without a hitch – as indeed usually the whole line does – and finally I throw to hounds the worry, which Jack has handed me, blow 'the kill', and after exchanging courtesies with those who have taken part, take the road with the hounds and whips for the long, but in spite of all, contented hack back to the kennels. Another day with the drag will soon be over. But I tell myself at the end that it is Bella, not I, who is the hero, or rather the heroine, of it all. And the cosseting which she receives on arriving at the stables, after hounds have been delivered into the hands of the kennel-huntsman, makes this thoroughly clear.

A few weeks after this I was again making preparations for the following Wednesday's meet of the Drag. It was a particularly good line. An hour and a half's hack from kennels – I always liked this as it seemed to settle hounds down much better than a short hack or going in the van – and an excellent piece of country with three legs, each of about 2 miles. There was an interesting and demanding variety of obstacles – some stiffish posts-and-rails with a ditch one side, some splendid brush fences, a few gates and one marvellous uphill open ditch which never failed to thrill. By this time I knew all the farmers pretty well, and with my two companions – the runner and the chief of our fence-mending team – was walking each leg, checking on fences and the red-and-white direction signs, calling in on each farmer to remind him that we were coming – although they all got the meet notices, they liked a chat as well. As we walked, our driver took the Land Rover to pick us up at the end of a leg and take us to the start of the next one. All seemed well – fences in good order, the going just right, farmers happy. We ought to have a good day.

I was anxious that we should because an old friend had promised to come and have a day with us, and I had the loan of a goodish animal for him. There was only one fly in the ointment. My beautiful Bella had cut her knee while jumping a fence on the previous week's line and would not be fit for several weeks. I had a call on a large grey gelding called General who went well enough in a group, but I was not so sure whether he would lead over all the fences, and in the Staff College Drag it was necessary that the Master, who usually hunts hounds as well, should not have to struggle trying to make his horse jump. He must get out in front and stay there. Well, we would see.

Shortly before midday on the Wednesday we were both at the kennels, myself on General, my friend on Jasper. My two whips, both cadets, were already there, and after having a word with Jack and putting some pieces of bread in the pocket of my hunting coat, I signalled him to let the hounds out. We were taking five couple – among them I noticed Flyer and Driver, both lean, wild and mean. Hounds were coupled. I was taking no chances on the hack to the meet. We moved off at about quarter past twelve. We always met at 2 p.m. and would be there with some ten minutes to spare. I must confess that even after having done the job for some time, I always enjoyed the hack back better than the hack there. You can never quite rid yourself of the butterfly feeling. It is not that you are particularly anxious for your own skin, but rather that you do not want anything to go wrong and spoil the day for all the supporters.

All went smoothly to and at the meet. Hounds were uncoupled, girths tightened, old friends greeted, new ones made. There was a good field, nearly 30, not surprising as it was one of the best lines we had. We met at the drive entrance to a large country house. To reach the start of the first leg, we would have to turn left out of the gate. The runner with the 'smell' had been gone some twenty minutes when I blew the customary short note on the horn and we moved off. Imagine my consternation when, after we had jogged a few hundred yards down the road towards the laying-on point, a fox, yes, a large brown dog fox, slunk across the road without so much as a glance at me or the hounds, down into a ditch and up again into the adjoining field. I was speechless with amazement and apprehension. Behind me members of the field, including my friend on Jasper, were less inarticulate. Every form of oral encouragement was hurled at the fox, at my hounds and at me.

There are those who will tell you that the natural instincts of draghounds have been ruined by strong, false scents and that they are no good for anything but following a smell. Be wary of such assurances. My draghounds, with Flyer and Driver to lead them, would hunt anything – a panther, a rhinoceros or a wild boar. Certainly they had no doubts about our uninvited guest. Giving tongue with unaccustomed vigour and volume, they surged forward in full cry. What was I to do? Let nature take its course or try to proceed with our planned jaunt across a prepared piece of country? Trollope's words nagged at me – 'he must condescend to no explanation and yet must impress men with an assurance that his decision will certainly be right'. Now, if ever, was the moment to make the right decision. In the event it was made for me.

It was made by M. Renard who re-crossed the road and, wonder of wonders, began to follow the laid line, seduced perhaps by a scent even more powerful than his own. There was no hesitating now. With a feeling of deep relief, accompanied by mounting excitement, I blew the 'gone away', turned left into the field where the line began, and galloped off after my hounds who were streaking in the wake of M. Renard. Just what he did while we were negotiating the next few fields and fences I never knew, for when we got to the end of the first leg, the hounds checked there, just as on a normal day. M. Renard had legged it. After a pause, having checked that the runner had moved on to the second leg and having got the hounds firmly under control with the aid of the whips, I exchanged a word with my friend who was as pleased with Jasper's performance as I was with General's. We moved off again.

There was about a mile to hack between the end of the first and the start of the second leg. All proceeded according to plan until the moment came when I released hounds into the field where the second leg began. Hounds immediately got on to the scent and were away. In the act of raising the horn to my lips, I saw out of the corner of my eye a herd of cows getting ready to stampede across my bows. Was it possible? Mr Bellamy was the most reliable of farmers. He never forgot when we were coming, never failed to take wire down or remove his cows to another field. Yet there they were, in the very act of putting up a wall of beef between the Master and his hounds. I aimed General for the corner of the field, hoping to reach the post-and-rail fence before the leading heifer. Until that moment I had no idea that cows could move so fast. Perhaps the Westerns do not exaggerate after all. It was obviously going to be a tight thing. In the event, General did something he and I have never done before or since. We jumped a cow and fence at the same time. The rest of the second leg was almost dull by comparison. Nothing untoward happened. At the check, my friend congratulated me. 'I had no idea', he observed, 'that drag-hunting could be so dramatically exciting.'

What can I say about the third leg? Only that we did not encounter an elephant during it. No circus riders or highwaymen or Cossacks appeared to disturb us. It was almost distressingly uneventful. Yet General took the open ditch in fine style. As we hacked home later, I noticed that even Flyer and Driver were somewhat subdued. Had they too been aware that we had had a very special day. My friend on Jasper had a final comment: 'You may call drag-hunting second best but even so you're finishing a very best second.' I had nothing to say in reply. My heart and my hands – for one can never tell with draghounds – were too full.

2

The Chase

See! how they range
Dispers'd, how busily this way and that
They cross, examining with curious nose
Each likely haunt. Hark! on the drag I hear
Their doubtful notes, preluding to a cry
More nobly full, and swell'd with every mouth.

Somerville

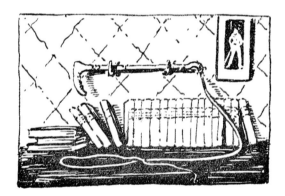

It may be doubted whether many of those at present wrestling so passionately with their sentiments about hunting, either one way or the other, know much of the origins or history of the sport. We are all aware of how devotedly William, Duke of Normandy pursued the deer and enlarged the New Forest – a former Saxon royal hunting ground – better to do so; and how severe were the laws against poaching, whether in the King's forests or the enclosures of lords and gentry. The year 1389 is a good starting point, when Chaucer is writing *Canterbury Tales* and Richard II's Parliament is complaining that 'artificers and labourers, and servants and grooms keep greyhounds and other dogs, and on the holy days, when good Christian people be at Church, hearing divine service, they go hunting in parks, warrens and coneyries of lords and others, to the very great destruction of the same'. Indeed so avidly did men of all classes, whether gentry, priests, farmers or labourers, go hunting or poaching that the Commons decreed that 'no layman with less than forty shillings a year in land, and no priest or clerk with less than ten pounds income a year [could] be so bold as to keep sporting nets or dogs'. How much notice was paid to this decree was another matter. Chaucer anticipated the poacher turned gamekeeper badge of efficiency by observing that 'a thief of venison . . . can kepe a forest best of any man'.

No section of the community embraced the chase with more enthusiasm than the gentry themselves. As Trevelyan has told us, they spent much of their lives hunting the deer with horse and hound, flying hawks at pheasant, partridge and heron, or lying out at night to net the fox and the badger. This zest for hunting sprang naturally from the Englishman's love of the country itself and his affection for horses and dogs. In the times of the early Tudors, Henry VII and Henry VIII, the English gentry relished the rural life – as indeed they still do – and astonished foreigners who noted that every English gentleman 'flieth into the country', having no regard for cities and towns; and what was described as the joyful background of country life consisted of hunting and hawking, snaring and fishing, whether conducted with great show and pomp by those gracing castles and manor houses or more clandestinely by small farmers and cottagers.

Hunting itself in these days did not mean fox-hunting. M. Renard, thought of then as the red thief, was killed by farmers – although later, in Elizabeth's reign, there were parts of England where both fox and badger were 'preserved by gentlemen to hunt and have pastime withal'. But for Henry VIII and his court, 'venery'[1] meant hunting the deer on horseback, while deer poaching which was all too common was mostly done on foot. As for the poor hare, it was hunted by everyone whether mounted or not. The English were regarded by others in Europe as singular in their marked love of horses and dogs, and they kept large numbers of them of many

[1] I trust none of my readers will misconstrue the word, although I fear that in Henry VIII's case its other less virtuous meaning does apply.

sorts. But as Trevelyan points out 'the horse was still a cumbrous animal. The slim racer and hunter of eastern blood had not yet come in, and a gentleman's mount was still bred to carry a knight in his armour at full trot, rather than a huntsman at full gallop'. And the farm horse took his share of ploughing duty.

Deer-hunting was often confined to the enclosed deer parks which every manor house of distinction boasted. The park would be well provided with trees and enclosed by a high wooden pale. In describing what a hunting morning was like, Trevelyan reminds us of the hounds that Theseus boasted of to Hippolyta as 'being match'd in mouth like bells' and while he does not say so, no doubt their 'heads were hung With ears that sweep away the morning dew'. The hounds would chase the deer round the enclosures with the high-hatted nobs of the manor, male and female, together with their friends, following at a leisurely pace on horseback. This somewhat tame version of hunting the deer was not, however, the only one. There were great herds of red deer on the hills and moors of the north, the Pennines and the Cheviots on the borders of Scotland and England while in the south the forests and woods were alive with fallow deer – unwelcome guests when it came to assaulting the villagers' and lord of the manor's crops. Beyond the enclosures, one purpose of which was to keep the deer out, there were plenty of deer to be hunted across the open country, allowing horsemen to indulge in a more adventurous and noble pursuit of their quarry – 'at force' as it was known.

This love of being out in the open countryside with horse and hound, irrespective of the quarry or indeed whether there was one or not, has never changed and, it is to be hoped, never will. We only have to recall BB's[2] enchanting story of a Pytchley Fox – *Rufus*, who outwits all his enemies and lives happily ever after – and to note the sentiments of the young horsewoman, Pamela, who, as the New Year was born,

> . . . longed for the covert side and the music of hounds that had been silent for so long. Her greatest joy lay in the swinging gallops over the wide fields, sound of the horn on the winter airs, and the pink bobbing coats. She hunted, not because it was 'the thing', but because she loved the countryside and horses,

[2] BB, pseudonym of Denys Watkins-Pitchford, whose stories of birds and beasts, together with his woodcuts, have delighted so many of us. The book quoted from here is *Wild Lone*.

and the thrill of clearing an 'oxer' was the greatest thrill of all . . . She lived on the sunny side of the wall, and knew not many evil things; she was at peace in this world of clean winter airs. With a largeness of mind that became her well did she grasp and seize elemental things, the simple joys that knew no ageing or decay. To be across her mare and to feel the wind of speed surging in her ears; to listen (not without a pang) to the sorrowing weep of the horn by the covert side, those were to her the greatest delights.

Not without a pang! Here B.B. is echoing Anthony Trollope's estimate of what a master of hounds should be like – that he should, for example, have an assurance that a fox is the most precious of all living things, that his feeling for the fox has in it an intense tenderness and that his desire to preserve the fox is passionate. But, of course, in Tudor times there was no fox-hunting as Trollope understood and we understand the word. Then the fox was subjected to a far more savage fate – either dug, bagged and baited or slaughtered as vermin by peasants. It was, as already observed, the stag which in Tudor times was the great quarry of those addicted to hunting. It took the Civil War, with its widespread destruction of deer and the devastation of deer parks, to bring about a change, so that at the Restoration in 1660 when Charles II came into his own again, although stag-hunting did continue, in many parts of the country it was the fox which became 'the beast of the chase'.

Yet for the time being fox-hunting remained a very private pursuit. Gentlemen would keep their own pack of hounds and invite their sporting neighbours to join them in the chase. This in turn meant that the hunt was not confined to the woods, parks and farmland of the gentlemen in question, but was developing into a more general and capricious cross-country chase no matter whose land was ridden over. There were still no packs of hounds supported by subscriptions, which would have entitled the general public having the means and inclination to take part in the sport. But even though the ownership of hounds remained private, there was emerging a need for wider management and organisation of the hunt if the desired effect was to be achieved. For example, in some counties it was the custom that earths should be stopped so that the fox could be hunted in the open and thus long runs of 10 miles, even 20, enough to test the boldness, skill and stamina of hound, horse and rider alike to the full, could be enjoyed. On the other hand, elsewhere, in Lancashire for instance, the idea was to get the fox to go to earth, so that he could then be dug out. One hunting man of the later Stuart period recalled that during a day's hunting at Sullom, they 'found two foxes, but could get neither of them to earth'. Such an admission supports the view of another writer that 'the hunters ran a fox to earth and then dug him out; if he refused to go to earth he generally got away'. As he also commented, such a method of hunting indicated that the hounds concerned were not bred with a view to tirelessness.[3]

Lady Mary Wortley Montagu, the celebrated blue-stocking, letter-writer, poet and friend of Alexander Pope (with whom she later quarrelled) had some unkind things to say about these hard-drinking foxhunters of the manor house, describing them as being 'insensible to other pleasures than the bottle and the chase'. She was speaking about the squires of a county in the south of England, and one of her grievances was that the females of such families were not permitted a coach because their lords and masters had no use for such contrivances, their time being wholly absorbed with hounds by day and with 'as beastly companions' by night, together with as much liquor as they could get. It was not an altogether fair portrait for country gentlemen could be scholarly and learned[4] as well as addicted to hunting. Nor should we overlook the sporting and social propensities of the very females with whom Lady Mary is sympathising. One of our Restoration dramatists puts these words into the mouth of a lively girl: 'I can gallop all the morning after the hunting horn and all the evening after a fiddle. In short I can do everything with my father but drink and shoot flying'.[5]

As the eighteenth century got underway the people of England certainly lived life to the full, and in speaking of those who did so, having both means and opportunity, we must distinguish between the ladies and gentlemen of fashion, who graced such places as London, Bath and

---

[3] We will see later what Peter Beckford has to say about the breeding of hounds.

[4] A rural squire, to crowds and courts unknown
 In his own cell retired, but not alone;
 For round him view each Greek and Roman sage,
 Polite companions of his riper age.

Somerville, 'The Chase'

[5] Silvia in George Farquhar's *The Recruiting Officer* (1706). To 'shoot flying' became common in Charles II's reign, and was regarded as difficult, the more so when practised from horseback.

Tunbridge Wells, and the country squires and their families of the manor house. For those in town the gaming table, with its lure of cards and dice, figured more largely than for the sporting and farming squire who was more obsessed by his stables and kennels. Yet both men and women of fashion *and* the rural gentry gambled freely, with the result that huge sums of money would change hands, a condition that the less fortunate found hard to reconcile to the expense involved in keeping up an estate, let alone improving it with building, planting, laying out gardens or introducing new agricultural methods. If gaming were confined to those with the wherewithal to indulge in it, the same could not be said of drunkenness which, Trevelyan maintains, 'was the acknowledged vice of Englishmen of all classes'. For the common folk this meant ale until, later in the century, cheap spirits rivalled it and the days of 'Drunk for a Penny, Dead Drunk for Twopence' were depicted by Hogarth's horrifying drawings. For the upper classes the tipple was either ale or wine, and whether by a St James's Street gamester or a fox-hunting squire, both were heavily imbibed, although it may be supposed that recovery from such excess was more readily accomplished by the latter solely because of his habit of outdoor exercise.

Leaving aside this indulgence in gambling and drinking – which in turn, of course, led to quarrelling and duelling – the Englishman's other great and more wholesome addiction was to sport. England's bowling greens were the wonder and envy of all foreigners who saw them, so green and smooth were they, while in villages during Queen Anne's reign a rude kind of cricket was being played, as well as the far longer-established game of football. Cockfighting in little amphitheatres provided frenzied scenes of betting and shrieking for the encouragement of a favoured cock. But surpassing even this for spectacles of unbridled enthusiasm, excitement and partisanship was the sport of horse racing, which in Anne's day was largely conducted at local county meetings, where not only those horses in the race took part, for, as Trevelyan tells us, 'the spectators, most of them on horseback, galloped up the course behind the race, yelling with excitement'. It was not just the gentry who loved racing. At Newmarket, where the Stuarts had established the first national meetings, 'the vast company of horsemen on the plain at a match contains all mankind on equal footing from the Duke to the country peasant. Nobody wears swords, but are clothed suitable to the humour and design of the place for horse sports. Everybody strives to out-jockey (as the phrase is) one another'. It was at this time too (1711) that Ascot racecourse was laid out and Godolphin and his fellow patrons of racing introduced Arab and Barb blood to English horseflesh with profound consequences for the future of Britain's and indeed the world's Thoroughbreds.[6] No longer would the gentleman's mount be a cumbrous animal to carry the knight in armour at the trot, but would become the slim racer and hunter of eastern blood. Nor was this new character and appearance of England's horses to be exclusive to those indulging in sporting activities. Apart from them, for 'the upper and middle class riding was the commonest act of the day'. But as the eighteenth century advanced, so did the need for heightened qualities for both horse and rider engaged in the chase.

By this time the hunting of deer was declining and being replaced by fox-hunting. Indeed, the great herds of deer that had been wont to run wild in the forests and wastes of England had steadily decreased as the land was enclosed, the forests cut down and the demands of agricultural production grew more vocal. Yet fox-hunting had not yet overtaken hare-hunting in its popularity. We read, for example, that in 1835 there were 138 packs of harriers compared with 101 packs of foxhounds. The appeal of hare-hunting – now known as beagling – may readily be understood, as the circular course generally run by the hunted hare was easier to follow and view on foot than the long, straight run of the fox. Nevertheless, then as now, the fox-hunting field did include a pedestrian element. But the sheer enchantment of the hunt, with its horses, hounds and hunting horn, red or blue coats, the thrill, speed and hazard of the chase, fired the imagination of all countrymen – and women too – so that 'spirited fox-hunting songs were shouted as loudly and as joyously on the ale bench as round the dining table of the manor'. And, no doubt, then as now too, those taking part in a glorious run vied with one another in recounting the fearsome double-oxers, the daunting five-barred gates, the wide, deep brooks and other tricky fences they had successfully negotiated.[7]

[6] English Thoroughbreds descend in direct male line from three Arabian strains – Byerly Turk, Darley Arabian and Godolphin Arabian.

[7] As Somerville put it:
    with emulation fired
    They strain to lead the field, top the barred gate,
    O'er the deep ditch exulting bound, and brush
    The thorny-twining hedge.

By the second half of the eighteenth century, when the third of the Hanoverian kings, Farmer George, was on the throne, fox-hunting had advanced to conditions which we would readily recognise today. No longer an affair of riding to hounds over your own lands and those of your neighbours and friends, hounds would now hunt over whole districts and 'great Hunts like the Badminton[8], the Pytchley and the Quorn carried the science to the point where it has remained ever since'. Long runs with numerous fences – for the famous hunting shires, like Leicestershire and Rutland, had, since the Enclosure Act, divided up the formerly open fields with formidable hedges – were the order of the day and made great demands on the quality, courage, staying power and jumping skills of the horses and on the boldness, nerve and horsemanship of those riding them.

Although Anthony Trollope tells us somewhat cynically that no hunting man ever wants to jump if he can help it – for some hedges were not exactly alluring – and men would often rather go for little hunting gates 'poking and shoving each other's horses, and hating each other with a great bitterness of hatred', yet those of us who have completed a run with a number of nasty-looking obstacles behind us know that without the challenge and exhilaration that went with them, it could hardly be counted as a run at all. Indeed Trollope's own exploits in the hunting field give the lie to his words. In his *Autobiography* he describes his hunting in Essex – where he lived from 1859 to 1871 – as the chief scene of his sport, and confesses to many falls. Few, he declares, have investigated the depth, breadth or water-holding capacity of Essex ditches more closely than he has, but through it all he was sure that Essex men would concede that he had ridden hard. He admits to knowing very little about hunting, for his poor eyesight prevented him seeing hounds or their quarry. At least he tried to ensure that he did not ride over hounds. Fences he would ride at without comprehending their nature, so that he would either follow another horseman or ride at them quite convinced that he could end up in a horse-pond or a gravel-pit and often did! Yet he continued to ride hard across country, taking fences as they came, hating roads, despising those who stuck to them, and 'feeling that life can not, with all her riches, have given me anything better than when I have gone through a long run to the finish, keeping a place, not of glory, but of credit, among my juniors'. How

[8] Now the Beaufort.

fully we would all endorse his sentiments, and might too observe that drag-hunting would have suited Trollope for a good run with plenty of fences would be guaranteed and these fences would be so arranged that there was *not* a horse-pond or a gravel-pit on the far side. There is no record of Trollope having been out with a pack of draghounds, although he could have done so, for in 1855 the Cambridge University Drag Hunt was established, with kennels at Cherry Hinton. It is one of the oldest in the country; indeed its present Joint Masters would claim *the* oldest, but those dignitaries at present in charge of the Oxford Draghounds would point out that records of the Oxford University Draghounds – from which the presently named pack was formed – stretch back to the early part of the nineteenth century. There will be more to say about these and other packs of draghounds later.

Cambridge University Drag Hunt

Trollope would also have been sympathetic to one particular feature of drag-hunting which has, throughout its history, exercised a great appeal. It furnished an indubitable, challenging ride across country, with the hounds on parade, lots of jumping and all the ceremony of the meet, laying on,

54

gone away, a check or two, away again and a finale – all within a *minimum of time*. And time is precious. Trollope himself found it so precious that he would get his manservant to wake him at 5 o'clock in the morning in order to get a chapter or two of his current novel written before getting on with the other work of the day.

We should be grateful that he did, for his books are full of hunting scenes and no one described a nineteenth-century one better than Trollope. Surtees, for all his brilliance, invention, gift for description, candour and humour, presents us with a caricature of hunting and its people. Trollope gives us the real thing. Let us accompany them both to a meet.

Whenever Trollope writes of hunting his love of the sport instantly shines through. 'Of all sights in the world there is, I think, none more beautiful than that of a pack of fox-hounds seated, on a winter morning, round the huntsman, if the place of meeting has been chosen with anything of artistic skill.' By this he means a small, grassy field with neat, clipped hedgerows, with trees and farm buildings nearby and a certain unevenness of ground to mark the place where the hounds and hunt servants should position themselves. Trollope is not speaking here of a grand lawn meet in front of the magnificent house of some nobleman – however necessary such things might be to the sport – but rather of a small village with a few cottages and an old church, and nearby a 6- or 7-acre field in which the hounds felt thoroughly at home and where there was space enough for the huntsman to walk his horse up and down with hounds clustered round him should he wish to prevent them becoming chilled by too much sitting. To this idyllic scene are come the horsemen, changing their hacks for their hunters, chatting and – yes, in those days smoking[9], giving instructions to their grooms and generally preparing for the day ahead. The field contains country gentlemen, sporting farmers, officers from the local garrison, and lookers-on in their dog-carts and gigs. And then comes the Master himself, having been assisted on to his horse – for he is more than 70 – trotting off to his hounds and grunting somewhat roughly to those temerarious enough to address him. A mild, courteous man when not in the saddle, as a Master of Hounds he is able to exercise a tyranny which no one will care to dispute – provided he is successful. In comparing an MFH to the captain of

[9] Cigars, of course.

a ship, Trollope points out that the latter has supreme power over his men in that he can flog them or lock them up or stop their grog, whereas a Master of Hounds is obliged to rely on the use of sharp words to stop the tongue or horse of any offender. We will leave him there as, with a final 'Gentlemen, the hounds can't get out if you will stop up the gate', he moves off to draw a nearby wood.

It is a familiar, agreeable picture, one that will jog the memory of many. How different a portrait is sketched for us by Surtees when he writes of a day with Mr Puffington's hounds to which Mr Sponge had been invited! To start with, the meet is at Hanby House where everything is in apple-pie order, the trim lawns swept clean of capricious stray leaves, the gravel rolled and cleared of all former hoof and wheel marks, the hunt breakfast being prepared for those gentlemen staying in the house, who, in demolishing the splendid spread on table and sideboard, were ably assisted by a bustle of further sportsmen arriving shortly before the advertised time of the meet. Then, just before 11 o'clock, Mr Bragg the huntsman appears with his hounds. 'They were just gliding noiselessly over the green sward, Mr Bragg rising in his stirrups, as spruce as a game-cock, with his thoroughbred mare gambolling and pawing with delight at the frolic of the hounds, some clustering around him, others shooting forward a little, as if to show how obediently they would return at his whistle.' Mr Bragg is one of those men whose politeness is measured according either to the rank of the other party or to the magnitude of his tip. A peer would receive a great sweep of his cap, a baronet half as much, a mere knight a quarter; or, again, a large tip yielded a lordly salute, a middling one caused an adjustment of his cap, a small tip no more than a forefinger to its peak, no tip a bleak stare. On Mr Bragg's appearance 'the men all began to shuffle to the passage and entrance-hall to look for their hats and whips; and presently there was a great outpouring of red coats upon the lawn, all straddling and waddling, of course'. Thereupon Mr Bragg musters his forces and, facing the assembled company, salutes the field with a generous sweep of his cap. He then informs Mr Puffington that it is past eleven and that they should be moving, and when Puffington, in reply to a question, announces that they will draw Rabbitborough Gorse, Bragg at once contradicts him and declares that he is going first to Hollyburn Hanger. Whatever Puffington had said would have prompted an instant rebuff from Bragg. Meanwhile the gentlemen have rushed to their horses, scrambled up with lots of 'fidgetings, and funkings, and *who-o*-hayings and drawing of girths, and taking up of curbs, and lengthening and shortening of stirrups'. And so, under the generalship of Mr Bragg, away they go.

In some ways Surtees, although himself an MFH, was a curious chronicler of hunting. He disliked fashionable society, he was prejudiced and prickly, feared no man, eschewed cant, and reveals an aspect of hunting very different from that of the more genial Trollope. They had this in common, however; they both loved the sport. It is also the case that during the lifetime of them both, drag-hunting started.

3
State of the Game

'Trail scents began as foxhound contests which could be easily watched as one hunt pitted their prowess against another. It was not long before people realised it would be fun to follow on horseback and enjoy the fast and furious pursuit.'

Lin Jenkins

There are at present[1] sixteen packs of draghounds in Great Britain and the Channel Islands, and one of them well to the fore is the Berks and Bucks, who have been good enough to provide a comprehensive account of their origins and activities. This pack of draghounds was the inspiration of Roger Palmer who is still Chairman. He was originally very keen on beagling and had founded his own pack, the Palmer Milburn Beagles, in 1971 in country not previously hunted by them. But having found it difficult to raise enough support for this form of sport and having observed while at Cambridge that the Trinity Foot Beagles and Cambridge

[1] *Baily's Hunting Directory*, 1998–99. See page 194 for a list of drag hunts.

University Draghounds shared kennels, he decided to do something similar, and in 1974 started the Berks and Bucks. This coalition worked well for whereas the draghounds took much time and money to run, there was such enthusiastic support for them that funds flowed in; on the other hand the beagles demanded relatively modest financial backing and, even this, because of limited following, was not easy to raise. So the two activities complemented each other admirably. Even so, there were serious problems before the hunt got going. To get things off the ground Teresa Whitworth – who was Master from 1976 to 1979 – together with friends, organised the first of many Aniseed Balls in London on St Valentine's Day, which produced enough money to get going, and the first meet at Appleshaw was in December 1974 when expenditure on stirrup cups exceeded cap takings, a circumstance clearly characteristic of this most enterprising drag hunt. Indeed their activities and initiatives are of such interest that they deserve to be fully described.

Beginning with a few hounds, some of which were black and tan from Dumfriesshire – generously given by Sir Rupert Buchanan-Jardine – they soon found that it was no easy matter to teach draft foxhounds, which, after all, had only been drafted in the first place because of unsatisfactory performance, to hunt an artificial scent. The scent chosen was nothing if not original, for wolf droppings supplied by the Master's tame wolves, smartened up by some additional ingredients, made what the Hunt called a good cocktail[2]. In any event, because of this initial failure rate with the hounds, they determined to breed their own[3] and now have an unusually large number of hounds in kennels, 25 couple, nearly all black and tan, with an occasional showing of white, and predominantly Dumfriesshire and Scarteen. This breeding venture has been a great success.

A further difficulty of the Hunt's early days was where to kennel the hounds. At first Roger Palmer kept them at his parents' home and looked after them himself. This meant getting up frightfully early each morning to exercise them before setting off for London and work at the still early hour of 7 o'clock. It also meant that there was no one to see to the hounds for the rest of the day, and they began to fight. This unhappy state of affairs was brought to an end by an absurd misadventure which came about when

---

[2] The formula is secret.
[3] See page 114 for our, the 4th Hussars', own venture into the world of breeding.

he was exercising hounds on a bicycle and was crossing a bridge over the M4 motorway. A fox suddenly appeared[4] and, reaching the far side of the bridge, ran alongside the motorway for several furlongs before bolting down a drain. Hounds, of course, were in hot pursuit with Roger Palmer, dismounted by now, chasing behind them, shouting, and being as totally ignored as I had been when my hounds used to go spare on Barossa Common. Fortunately the hounds too went down the drain and were safely mustered on the far side. A change was clearly called for. The new kennels behind Windsor High Street, however, were hardly more successful, for Colin Lisle, hacking the hounds along the High Street, was unable to prevent one of them raiding a butcher's and emerging with a string of sausages – not just once, but on several occasions. Another move was indispensable.

In fact two more moves were necessary, first to a temporary home at Lady Waverley's near Goring Heath, where the beagle kennels were and so enabling the kennel-huntsman there, at that time Philip Cole, to look after the draghounds too. Then, in 1979, the draghounds actually moved into the beagle kennels, and this arrangement lasted until 1982 when, finally, the Hunt's own new purpose-built kennels were established at Lambourn Woodlands to house both packs. The hunting itself, the most important part of the game, benefited greatly when Ian Balding became one of the Joint Masters in 1977, for not only did he bring with him, as it were, the Kingsclere-Baughurst country south of Newbury, which became the central part of the Hunt country, but he guaranteed that the fences would be of the highest quality. His own horsemanship and boldness across country are legendary and a model for all, as is his skilful concern in dealing with loose horses. He has been President of the Hunt since 1996.

The Berks and Bucks Draghounds meet on Sunday and Wednesday, indeed they were the first pack to hunt on a Sunday – now six other drag hunts do. Their country is extensive, and lines are hunted by courtesy of the local foxhounds in Berkshire, Buckinghamshire, Hampshire, Oxfordshire and Wiltshire. There are some seventeen different meets for the 26 Sundays of the season and for occasional Wednesdays. A normal day's line will cover about 10 miles, and may be broken down into as many as six legs, depending on the number of fences, of which there must be a

[4] See my comparable encounter with a fox, page 44.

minimum of 45 over 95 per cent grassland. Some lines have 90 fences – an exceptionally high number. The Berks and Bucks have always placed great emphasis on the quality of their fences, and for this purpose they buy a triple-width amount of hedge saplings, planted double spacing, and so they grow a big double-hedge fence with a small alternative beside it. As the Hunt points out, this emphasis on having easier, alternative fences pays off, for the lead horses, knowing that there is a more simple option, will clear the larger fence quite happily, and, of course, the horseman or horsewoman too, aware of the less daunting alternative, will ride at their fences with confidence – and, as we all know, boldness in a rider quickly communicates itself to the horse. These fences vary from post-and-rails, ditches and tiger traps to formidable hedges up to 5 feet. But to ensure that most of the field finish the line successfully, the Hunt makes it plain whether a particular meet is, or is not, suitable for novices. There is one other very special feature of the Berks and Bucks Draghounds – they go back to the origin of a trail scent (see Lin Jenkins at the head of this chapter) and organise trail races for their hounds at country shows. Full marks to the Berks and Bucks!

While most drag hunts have much in common – the dedication and hard work of those in charge, dependence on the goodwill of farmers and landowners, a need to keep finances in order, care for the provision and maintenance of proper fences, devotion to horse and hound, sound selection of hunt servants, a demand for boldness in horse and rider, plus love of the sport and the sheer fun of it – yet there are notable differences between them too. The Isle of Man Hunt has three and a half couple of bloodhounds, a very modest subscription, relatively low fences, none more than 3 foot 6 inches, all marked, small fields and their country covers the whole island, which has no other kind of hunting. By way of contrast, the North East Cheshire has 26 couple of hounds – the only drag hunt with more than the Berks and Bucks; Cambridge University will sometimes have a field of 100; the subscription for two hunts is more than £300; the Mid-Surrey Farmers stress the importance of fielding 'a good brave horse and rider as hedges jumped in a day go from thirty to eighty and are around 4'6" to 5' plus a ditch'. This last point, of course, applies to drag-hunting generally.

There are other features which many packs have in common. Most of them favour kennels of some six to ten couple; the majority hunt on Saturday with an occasional Wednesday, while Sunday comes a good second; lines of 8 to 10 miles in all, with checks between different legs[5], are normal; many drag hunts were formed during the last 25 years or so, although a few originated in the nineteenth century. (The list on page 194 shows which ones.)

The most revealing comments about a particular hunt come from those concerned, and there is perhaps room here for some of them. John Lee has long been the driving force behind the West Shropshire Hunt, and he explains that, in 1981, when fox-hunting ceased there, he took it over as a private pack and it became a drag hunt. Having told his hunting friends what he proposed to do and having also taken advice from the North East Cheshire, which had been established since 1958, he mustered 32 supporters for his first season, 1981–82, and as he writes: 'We opened up the country substantially and on an average day we would have 5 or 6 lines[6] and jump 35–45 fences, covering a distance of two miles on each line. The hounds that we drafted from various hunts took to draghunting very well.[7] We ended up with 8 couple, which we find is a good number for a Drag Hunt.' John Lee goes on to tell us that his former huntsman, Ken Williams, had bought a cottage in their country, kennels were built and he looked after the hounds for the first three seasons. Later they moved hounds to the Tanatside kennels. They also decided after three seasons to change to a bitch pack only and found this much more successful for drag-hunting. During their second season John Lee's son joined him as Joint Master, and while father continued to hunt hounds, son became Field Master. While Jonathan, the son, continues as a Joint Master, John Lee himself is now Chairman and Secretary of the Hunt, so that it remains very much a family affair. They have excellent country thanks to the help of adjacent hunts, with good hedges and post-and-rail fences, meet on Saturday, with an occasional Thursday bye-day, and, with a membership of 50, usually have a field of 25 to 30. Their first point-to-point at Weston Park was a great success in 1985, and since then has continued not only to be very enjoyable, but profitable too.

[5&6] Nomenclature varies. I was taught that a *line* would have several *legs*. Others call *each* part of a day's course a line.

[7] See the Berks and Bucks, page 59, who had to breed their own.

Another great success story is that of the Mid-Surrey Farmers' Drag hounds, which originated in the mid-1920s with kennels at Epsom, and was known then as the Banstead Drag, later the Mid-Surrey. Disbanded at the outbreak of the Second World War, the hunt was revived for the 1947–48 season with its present name, and among those who started it up again were the Hon. Philip Kindersley – who was Chairman until 1996, when he handed over to the Hon. Mr Justice Cazalet – and Alan Skinner, who recalled that the first meet at The Hoskins, Oxted was chaotic, with hounds all over the place and no proper control. It was very much a small, élite club, and even now attendance is limited to members, with visitors taking part only with the Master's permission. When the Drag was first re-started they had Fell hounds and found them far too fast! Since then they have changed to foxhounds. Some of the meets are organised in the East Sussex and Southdown country by one of the Joint Masters, David Robinson, who 'believes in having the longest and biggest lines'. Indeed some members can recall legendary days with such long and huge lines that *three horses* were needed, and one particular member was instructed to go only half-way because he had only one horse. We have already noted the number of fences (30 to 80) and their height (up to 5 feet) and with average fields of 20 or so, 'we may be mad,' a member notes, 'but we enjoy ourselves and always have super teas afterwards and discuss the day's dragging and see who has a dirty back with lots of joking'.

In writing of drag-hunting, we tend to emphasise the horses, the hounds, the country, the riders and those who prepare everything and allow their land to be ridden over, but we should never forget the indispensable 'runner' who drags the scent – the 'smell' – over the line and so makes the hunt possible. In my regiment it was done by a captain, fit and fleet of foot; at the Staff College by a Sandhurst cadet; at Cambridge by an athletic undergraduate. Hounds usually hunt an aniseed scent, although Cambridge once used panther's urine from London Zoo, and the runners were known as 'panthers'.

At the head of this chapter are some words written by Lin Jenkins which appeared in a most readable and timely article published by *The Times* in December 1997. The occasion prompting this article was an invitation she had accepted to take part in a drag hunt over HRH The Prince of Wales's land at Highgrove, and we will come to her description and comments about it shortly. She was mounted on a fourteen-year-old gelding, a grey

Cambridge University Drag Hunt

named Toffee, who had been brought up properly by having had several seasons with the Staff College Drag[8] about which I have already had something to say. Lin Jenkins supplemented her account with a short piece explaining the origins of drag-hunting and offering advice to the uninitiated about, as she put it, 'how to join the Victorian sport of drag-hunting'. She reiterates the point I made earlier that the sport developed because of the sheer convenience to those horsemen and horsewomen who wanted the fun of riding to hounds across country with a number of testing obstacles, but who did not have the time or patience to hunt conventionally and put up with the disappointment of waiting about all day and not enjoying a run at all. As already recorded, Oxford University was one of the first to form and hunt a pack of draghounds, followed by

[8] In my day Sandhurst Foxhounds and Staff College Drag; now Staff College and Royal Military Academy Sandhurst Draghounds.

Cambridge and then the Army. For the soldier, of course, the drag's coalition of relatively little time needed for the sport and the intensity of excitement, even danger, had a very special appeal, with the result that the Shorncliffe Drag was established in east Kent in 1861. Two years later the Household Brigade started a pack of draghounds, to be followed in turn by the Royal Artillery in 1866, based at Woolwich. Then, in 1870, officers of the Staff College, together with the staff and cadets of Sandhurst, formed their own private pack. It flourishes today. Indeed, the Staff College Drag has had some celebrated masters and whips. After being disbanded in 1939, it was restarted by that lovable character, Mick Lindsay of the King's Dragoon Guards, while a student there, and he rekindled the wonderful spirit and dash that the Hunt had enjoyed in the days of Dick McCreery, who had whipped-in ten years before the war and, to many, was the greatest cavalry soldier of his time. Other masters, many of them celebrities of the equestrian world, are too numerous to name, but they included such men as Bill Lithgow, Charles Coaker, Robert Ferguson,

*Staff College
Drag Hounds
1895/6*

Monkey Blacker, John Riley – who also ran the Jersey Draghounds – John Mogg, Piers Bengough, Maurice Johnston, Arthur Douglas-Nugent and a host of others. Their time in office was necessarily short, because of moving on to other appointments, but with such men in charge it may readily be seen that the fun was furious and the sport exhilarating. Long may it last.

In describing her day out with the drag at Highgrove, Lin Jenkins explains that this part of the Gloucestershire pasture is rich in well-trimmed hedges and properly maintained drystone walls, both of which she and Toffee encountered early on. Having observed a horse and rider in front of her do serious damage to a well-manicured hedge, taking it by the roots, leaving a large-sized hole in it and plummeting down the far side into a ditch in a crumpled heap, she decided to close her eyes and leave it all to Toffee. His successful negotiation of the hedge, however, could not rid her of some apprehension as they approached the first drystone wall of the line. Hedges can be brushed through, gates will give way, post-and rails may be scraped over, but stone walls are different. She had been warned not to attempt to fly them – the show-jumping technique of steadying and collecting the animal before hopping over was recommended. Lin Jenkins was not comforted by seeing another misjudged attempt to negotiate what is, after all, a rock-solid obstacle. Another member of the field, whose horse had misjudged the wall, taken off much too soon and crashed chest-first into it, certainly cleared it himself, but in doing so parted company with his mount and executed a forward roll on the far side. Lin was still trying to pass an urgent message to Toffee to the effect that for both their sakes he should slow down, and they were by now but three strides away. 'With a second to go, he finally responded to my desperate efforts and, sitting back on his hocks, cleared the wall in fine style. Then we were on to the next, and the next, even when the afternoon sun was so low in the sky that we could not see where we were going.' In short she had a terrific day.

While conceding that drag-hunting is 'immense fun' Lin Jenkins does not minimise its dangers, but then such hazards are common to all equestrian sports. If there were no element of danger, where would the excitement and the challenge be? Several of her fellow horsemen and horsewomen that day ended up with cuts and bruises, and worse – damage to their pride. Indeed, one woman elected to collide facially with a wall, but was still able to walk away before being transported to hospital.

Another of her companions was one of the most stalwart and hardworking supporters of drag-hunting, Brian Stern, who is Secretary of the Masters of Draghounds Association. Mounted on his 17.3 h.h. hunter, Jack, Brian sailed fast and smoothly over the Highgrove hedges, and, while confiding to Lin his unbounded enthusiasm for the sport, told her to remember that 'drag-hunting is a game'. Although HRH The Prince of Wales was not out himself on this occasion, he is no stranger to drag-hunting. As Pat Sutton[9], one of the great goers of the Staff College Drag, recalled, when Prince Charles was a student at Sandhurst he went out regularly with the hounds and, what is more, 'He always rode up at the front'. But even though he may not have joined in the fun that day, that he should have been the host

Staff College Drag Hounds 1895/6

[9] Pat Sutton, Joint Master and huntsman of the Staff College Draghounds since 1977; Chairman of the Masters of Draghounds Association. A widely acknowledged expert on drag-hunting, with unlimited enthusiasm for it, she has given me indispensable assistance with this book.

to a day's drag-hunting at Highgrove, a unique event at which the field was drawn from some eight packs of draghounds, gave a kind of royal accolade to the sport which may have some significance for the future. It is important *not* to see this as an implicit recognition that drag-hunting could be a substitute for the real thing – for nothing could do that – but rather as a great boost for the sport itself. As Brian Stern put it, being invited to meet at Highgrove was 'quite a coup'. Nor was the present heir to the throne the only one to give such wholehearted support to drag-hunting. His great uncle, HRH Prince Edward, was an enthusiastic rider to hounds, and enormously enjoyed those occasions when he went out with another military pack – alas no longer with us now – the Household Brigade Draghounds. So excellently have their activities been recorded in past *Journals* of the Household Brigade that they merit a chapter to themselves.

4

The Household Brigade Draghounds

All Melton the fox over pastures may follow!
All London may ride in the road with the stag!
All Brighton hunt hare – up hill – down hollow –!
But give me the devil's delight of the DRAG!!

Household Brigade Journal 1870

One of the first records of what were then called the Windsor Garrison Draghounds appears in the *Household Brigade Journal* of 1865, and notes that:

This capital pack had their first trial on Wednesday, the 25th October, at Harbour Hill, Slough, when Green, the celebrated runner, gave them some first-rate leaps over fences and ditches, taking the drag first over the white rails away to Eton Wick, across the meadows to Dorney Common, away to Mr Aldridge's, at Cippenham, by Two-mile Brook to Farnham Royal, leaving

Household Brigade Draghounds, Hawthorn Hill 1937

Stoke Park and finishing at Mr H Cantrell's Bayliss Farm, Stoke. Lord Earlsport was master, and Messrs Talbot and Thorold whips; most of the officers of the First Life Guards, and Grenadier Guards, and many of those of the Brigade in London, were out.

They could hardly have chosen a more auspicious day than 25 October. On that day only eleven years earlier had taken place the gallant, although mistaken, charge of the Light Brigade at Balaklava. And indeed, the Draghounds' next meet almost coincided with another great Crimean battle at which the Foot Guards so distinguished themselves, for it was on 11 November, only six days later than the battle of Inkerman, also in 1854. Moreover, it was a day that, because of a later, much bloodier and prolonged war, is remembered still and surely always will be 'while memory holds a seat In this distracted globe'. On this particular day in 1865 Mr Greville was in command of the Drag, remaining so for the rest of the season. They had a good run which finished in the Brocus to be received by a crowd of Etonians.

By following the fortunes of this particular pack, we may observe how what Lin Jenkins called the Victorian sport of drag-hunting progressed from the nineteenth century to the twentieth, and in doing so both enlighten those who know little of the sport and stir the memories of those fortunate enough to have enjoyed it. No two packs of draghounds are identical in character, country or clientele, but most of them have much in common, and it would be laborious to relate the activities of too many packs. The breeding of hounds may differ, numbers in kennels, the size of fields, length of lines, number and nature of fences in each line, day of meets, date of origin, uniform, subscription, type of country – all these may differ, but the essentials of keeping kennels sweet, hounds fit, farmers content, hunt servants keen, finances in order, subscribers happy, horses in drag-hunting trim, are features universally accepted and adhered to. Above all, everyone involved will wish to ensure that a day with the drag, no matter which one, will combine all the joy of riding over beautiful country, dressed in its autumn, winter and early spring colours, with a series of testing fences to encounter, hounds streaming away in front, and in the company of kindred spirits savouring the sheer pleasure of finishing well. These things are surely shared by all kinds and classes of people who love horses and who pursue the sport of drag-hunting.

Although, by selecting one particular version of events, we may forfeit the prize of being exhaustive, we may at least aspire to the felicity of being representative. And just as there are few differences of purpose, method, ceremony and general conduct among the various packs of draghounds that have existed or still do, so also we may say that, in these same respects, change between the centuries has not been great. What has changed are attitudes, personalities, participants, methods of getting to and from meets, and – simply because of an environmental revolution embracing railways, roads, urban sprawl, farming practices and the profusion of barbed wire – the country over which draghounds run. Moreover, the very fact that of the seventeen[1] existing packs of draghounds, as *Baily's Hunting Directory* shows, about half have been established within the last 30 years, whereas others which flourished in Victorian times are no more – this in itself means that those changes which have occurred are confined to a small number of packs.

Let us now take a closer look at our selected pack, known in the 1860s and early 1870s as the Windsor Garrison Draghounds, and later as the Household Brigade Draghounds, and see what notable runs were enjoyed – or by some endured.

We will start with two days in November and December 1867. On 17 November they met at Chertsey, and here at once we do detect a difference from such affairs today, for before they began the line a sumptuous lunch was provided by Mr Pilcher of the Hollies, for a large number of supporters, some of whom were officers from Windsor, Hounslow and London. The line itself ran from a meadow close to Chertsey, leaving Thorpe on the left, through Egham and on to Runnymede, then over the hills to Ouseley. The pace was furious and at the finish there were only three horsemen up with the hounds, the Master himself, Captain Ewart of the 2nd Life Guards, and two officers from Hounslow. Falls were numerous throughout the run, and one honourable gentleman, Mr Eykyn MP, had the misfortune to break his collar-bone. The December meet had many features in common. Again hospitality was provided, this time by Mr R. B. Harvey in 'true old English style' at the Langley Park meet, and there were lots of spectators from the neighbourhood, both at the meet and also at what were described as the two 'sensation jumps' – one of

---

[1] Sixteen in Great Britain and the Channel Islands; one in Ireland.

which, at the very start of the run, consisted of some 21 feet of water, complicated by furzed-up hurdles and a bank on the far side. This obstacle succeeded in bringing down five horsemen, but those who survived it went on by three farms to Upton Wood, then round by Langley Furze and back into the park, where the second 'rasping fence' had to be negotiated in order to finish in front of the house.

Some years later we come across what was described as one of the best days of the 1872–73 season. On 14 February an unusually large turnout mustered at Datchet Common, and a line of some 7 and a half miles had been selected, running to Horton, Colnbrook and West Drayton, then, after a check, across Stanwell Moor to Staines Moor and finishing at Staines railway bridge. 'The going was good, and the day beautifully fine. The fences and brooks, which were numerous, were stiff, and there were many casualties.' A few days later the Master, Lord Charles Innes Ker, brought his draghounds to Remenham House, Wyrardisbury – 'the hour was two o'clock; and punctual to the stroke of time Lord Charles Ker was at his post with the hounds, looking as fresh as paint, although they had had a long day so recently'. Again the field was lavishly entertained with a *déjeuner* organised by Mr Gordon Gyll. It was a capital refreshment and after all had partaken of it, hounds were laid on. The line took them over the Remenham farms to Staines Moor and then back again across some close country which presented numerous brooks and dykes to those taking part. It was some 6 miles in all, and as was customary Lord Charles was first up with the hounds at the finish, with two others in hot pursuit and the rest of the field strung out behind.

Between mid-October and late December 1879 the Household Brigade Draghounds, as they were now called, met fourteen times, mostly on Wednesdays and Saturdays, and they had some adventurous runs. The first meet of the season was, in fact, on a Thursday, 16 October, and a large field assembled at the Hind's Head, Touchen End. Early on in the run one enthusiast jumped his horse straight into a pond and had to swim for it; another animal elected to go through rather than over a gate and successfully demolished it while discomforting his rider. But perhaps the most dramatic incident sprang from the rivalry between a Grenadier Guardsman, Drummond, and a Prussian Guardsman, Count de Morella, who were vying for the lead when Drummond, unexpectedly confronted by a ditch into a lane, 'cast himself into it, much to the surprise and delight of his new purchase', thus allowing the Count to gain the advantage and finish in front. The account of this day records that the hounds went well together and that much to the disappointment of many expectant observers near the end of the line, Bone Brook was safely cleared by all those still up with the hounds.

At a Binfield meet in November the Draghounds were certainly able to provide 'five-and-twenty per cent' of what Mr Jorrocks called the danger of war. At the very first fence Captain Montgomery dismounted without permission, rapidly to remount however, while next Mr Brocklehurst came a cropper and was rolled over by his horse. Then, with hounds running very fast over Cabbage Hill, the pace was telling and when a huge upstanding fence with a big drop was gallantly charged by Mr Gough and Mr Foster, both came down, happily to get up again and rejoin the field when hounds checked two fields further on. The report of this day then makes mention of something quite foreign to anything we might expect to see today, for it tells us that 'after a *change of horses*' (my italics) 'a start was again made'. Second horses for a full day's hunting are common enough even now, but not for a day with the drag. But on they went, with Drummond having an argument with his horse, which was eventually resolved in his favour, and Mr Foster, again in trouble, seen to fall and be caught by his foot in the stirrup, then fortunately rescued by Mr Mildmay. Both were soon in pursuit of the flying pack, and the 7-mile line ended at the top of Brook Hill where 'the worry took place in front of Mr Overton's house'. It had been a great gallop, and it was noted that some members of the Staff College Drag, who had been out, acquitted themselves well. One more unusual event was to feature in an early January run, when the going was so deep in an 8-mile run that the dragman, Caley, was caught by the hounds and the Master, Mr Foster, had to whip them off. It was another day of numerous spills, none severe, but that, as we know, is part of the game.

Severe frosts during the early weeks of 1880 prevented hunting, but on 7 February the hounds met at Victoria Barracks, Windsor, and after luncheon a large field rode off to the steeplechase course where hounds were laid on. They streamed away at a furious pace over the racecourse, which produced a number of falls, through Captain Bulkeley's park, where Mr Grenfell had a nasty spill at a drop fence, then, after checking at the Rifle Butts, on again to Bone Brook – two more down here for the going was heavy – and so by New Lodge to finish at Mr Allnutt's farm. Mr Foster was still Master, with Mr Mildmay as whip who always seemed to ride well and finish well up with the hounds. A week later the hounds met at the Crown Hotel, Slough with a good field despite wet, miserable weather. After the line had taken them through Datchett there was a check at Horton, where – and here too we find a difference from present practices – the field was treated to entertainment in Mr John Graham's 'usual hospitable style', a feature of Victorian drag-hunting which would no doubt be welcomed today. Then on again to complete a line of some 7 miles with lots of good fences. Having lost some days early in the year, the Draghounds met frequently during the rest of the season, including two days when the field was entertained by Colonel and Lady Julia Follett, both great supporters, and at the first of these days, when the second part of the line ran from Egham to Chertsey, Lady Julia was the only one who finished with the hounds. All the others had come to grief. The Chertsey Brook frequently claimed its victims, and during the second day with the Folletts, Mr French, now whipping-in to Mr Beech, 'indulged in a cold bath'.

When hunting started again in the autumn of 1880, there were two meets at Holyport, at one of which there was a large detachment from the Staff College. We may note in passing here that many of those who have hunted with the Staff College Drag since the last war will be familiar with such places as Holyport, Winkfield, Hawthorn Hill and the Fifield Road, for this excellent line passed from the Household Brigade Draghounds to the Staff College during the post-war years. At the end of November 1880 Colonel Fraser and the officers, 2nd Battalion, Scots Guards entertained members of the Hunt at Victoria Barracks, and 'a large and fashionable company at luncheon' was able to enjoy music provided by the battalion's band. Then:

> ...the hounds were laid on near Bourne-lane, and ran over the old Steeplechase-course, crossing the Spital-road near the Kennels, and over the Clewer Lodge grounds, where they checked. The hounds were then trotted over the road and laid on again near the Windsor Racecourse, when they ran a good pace up the fields to Mr Thorn's farm, across the meadows to Dedworth Green, by the Butts, over Mr Winder's farm to Bullock's Hatch, and, crossing the big brook, which nearly all got over in safety, thence on by Fifield-lane to

Colonel Clayton's and Mr Alnutt's land, where they finished a capital line of nearly six miles. The land was very heavy, which caused many spills. Mr Astley, whip, came down very heavily after the check, but was soon remounted. The Master, Hon A Campbell, rode well throughout with his hounds, and was well up at the finish.

Such an account of a day with draghounds, enjoyed more than a hundred years ago, will still ring true in the minds of those pursuing the sport today, particularly for horsemen and women familiar with this part of the country. There are many features which both periods have in common – the nature of the field, although formerly with a larger military content, the length of line with checks, heavy going producing spills, absolute dependence on the goodwill of farmers and landowners, the need for the master to be well mounted and in control, the sheer good nature and fun of it all, enhanced by the attendant risk of negotiating a goodly number of obstacles, although I suspect that nowadays we have modified the severity of some fences, not only for the benefit of the horses, but also because today's management of land and farming has restricted the freedom of choice in taking a line across country. Another feature which will have its appeal for many of those connected with the British Army is that of the familiar and famous names of those who have served in the Household Cavalry and the Foot Guards for so many generations. I have tried not to weary the reader by listing too many of them, but, for me, to read of the exploits of those bearing such names as Fraser, Gooch, Brownlow, Seymour, Goulburn, Bulkeley and so on is to revive the good fortune that has been mine to know and serve with many of their descendants, and makes for me the relation of their adventures with the draghounds even more vivid and affecting.

Yet one more reminder of how things both do and do not change is presented to us when we read of a point-to-point taking place over a flagged course on Saturday 18 December 1880 under just the right sort of conditions, that is – horses to be the property of officers of the Household Brigade who are subscribers to the Drag; only horses that have never won any sort of race to be eligible; horses to be ridden in drag-hunting costume; all horses running to have been out with the Drag three times; hired horses allowed to run with the committee's approval; the whole of the sweepstake to go to the winner; the country to be selected by someone appointed by the committee; anyone going over 100 yards along a road or lane to be disqualified; stakes to be paid in advance; distance about 4 miles. What could be fairer or more sporting?

In the event, the course started at the village of Horton, then over 'Mr Graham's brook, round to Mr Stephen Pullin's, across the Bath-road to Riching's Park, and finished in Dr Southey's meadow near Mad Bridge'. There were nine starters, it was a good race, with plenty of casualties, and the order at the finish was first Mr Stacey, second Mr Abercromby, third Mr Astley. Today things are somewhat different, although it is good to note that at least half the current packs of draghounds have their own point-to-point. But you will hardly find any mention of going along roads and tracks now; the distance is more likely to be 2 to 3 miles, often run over what is virtually a racecourse, like Larkhill or Tweseldown; the horses will not always be owned by the riders, who will be wearing racing, rather than hunting, kit; while the prize money will be differently handled. But, happily, some point-to-points are still the real thing, over genuine drag-hunting country with those who have regularly hunted their own horses taking part. Long may the traditional way of doing it continue!

Whoever it was that wrote the notes recording the 1894–95 season of the Household Brigade Draghounds had a fluent pen and a proper acquaintance with Peter Beckford's great work. He tells us that for a meet on 12 December 1894, the Master brought nine and a half couple to the Red Lion, Southall, where a good field of officers from The Blues, Foot Guards and 8th Hussars, together with local sportsmen, assembled, and hounds having been laid on near Sudbury:

> . . . ran over a nice line of country to the Railway Bridge, where there was a temporary check; a cast worthy of one of Beckford's most inspired moments put hounds on the line the other side of the bridge. We then ran over some very nice fences on Mr Smith's farm, amongst which was a brook with some black palings on the take-off side. This fence our representative from the shires took great exception to, and declared that the like was not to be met with in any of the best countries; he displayed so rancorous a spirit towards it that he refused to leave it till he had levelled the palings to the ground, and desposited himself into the brook by way of a cooler.

There was a long run to the next check, and during it: 'our two celebrated jockeys, Slade and Murray-Threipland, who had hitherto ridden a waiting race, took advantage of it to execute a brilliant and punishing finish'. There were more unlooked-for snags in this line, when a farmer failed to leave a gate open, and only the first whip's initiative in finding a gap elsewhere managed to get the hounds back under control.

This entertaining scribe of ours delights us further with his account of a meet at Hawthorn Hill three days later, where Mr Benyon first provided a splendid lunch, during which everyone consumed a proper amount of what is entitled 'jumping powder' before moving off past the racecourse. During the first leg the second whip succeeded in falling into a road, which was the only fence not blessed with a good take-off and soft landing. Not to be beaten by the whip, when hounds were laid on again and ran over some good fences, the Master himself elected to take the last obstacle of this leg, a quickset hedge with a post-and-rails on the far side of the ditch in between, in such a manner that he landed his horse, Peterkin, with scientific precision *in* the ditch. Two weeks later the newly appointed Master, Steuart, brought eight and a half couple of hounds to Shottesbrook Park and did not have a happy time of it to start with, for when the hounds crossed a sunk fence and raced on, to the chagrin of all the field, not a single horse would face this same sunk fence, for they all seemed 'possessed with the same evil and obstinate spirit'. Have we not all despaired at one time or another when our normally bold and enthusiastic hunter has for no apparent reason jibbed at a fence and left us angry and frustrated, seeking a way round to catch up with the already distant draghounds? In this case we are told that:

> We rode sadly over the remainder of the line to the check in Mr Beal's meadow at Waltham St Lawrence, reflecting as we did so that had Mr Beckford devoted any part of his interesting work on hunting to the pursuit of the herring, he would have assuredly issued the following warning: 'Lay not on your hounds the wrong side of a sunk fence, unless you are certain that your horse is willing to convey you to the right side of it.'

Towards the end of the season there were to be more adventurous days. A meet at Old Windsor enabled the hounds to be laid on near Colonel Follet's, and although the first two fences were successfully negotiated by the field, at the third one, so fresh was the animal, that Pirate 'attempted the life of the Master; on being mildly asked to desist, he pulled back, but only to descend like an avalanche on the second whip at the next fence', an incident which prompted a comment that the life of a hunt servant is not a happy one! Later on in the line, one of the whips encountered an iron hurdle cunningly concealed in a hedge, happily without injury to either man or horse; another horseman appeared at the next check with a cigar in his mouth but no hat on his head, and when asked where it was, replied, 'In Northamptonshire' – his companions were well aware that his *heart* was in the 'shires', but could not imagine how his *hat* had got there. Nor was this all. The first brook of the last leg towards Chertsey effectively cried *finis* to one of the horsewomen out that day, and the business of rescuing her and her animal caused many of the field to lose the rest of the run.

It is rare for hounds to be late at a meet – although even in these days of supposedly reliable horse boxes and hound vans, they do sometimes fail us – yet such was the case on Wednesday 13 December 1895 when they arrived at the Yew Tree, Hedgerly somewhat after the appointed time. The explanation cleared the Hunt staff of recrimination, for the photographing of hounds and themselves had taken longer than expected. As if this were not enough, one of the nine and a half couple of hounds, Ranger, decided to make up for lost time and made off without permission, followed, despite all the Master's and whips' efforts (I know just how they must have felt) by the rest of the pack. The field were soon in pursuit, however, and the subsequent run over country that rode beautifully, with nice fences, was enjoyed by most of the field, except for Wyld, who, at a nasty drop fence, 'gave us a fine exhibition of gymnastics, turning no less than three somersaults in the air', and although Chester might not have been initially gratified at parting company with his horse while attacking the second fence, he may have changed his mind on observing 'the exceedingly heavy fall his riderless horse took at the next obstacle' from which 'he might not have escaped so easily'. In concluding his account of this particular day, the writer pays tribute both to the skill of the runner, Caley, and to some beautiful work by the hounds, who, in spite of poor scent on light fallow, would not – 'the flying beauties' – be shaken off. The finale to this eventful line was equally worthy of comment, for it seemed that Mr Howard-Vyse's beagles had been at the finish shortly before the draghounds arrived, and had 'with very puzzled faces been trying to make out what the nasty smell was and which way it was going'. The leading draghounds were not interested in the possibility of a hare. They preferred 'Caley's succulent worry'.

We may award the Household Brigade Draghounds full marks when we recall that they would meet as far afield as Amersham where, on Wednesday 20 March 1895, 'a long jog of sixteen miles brought the pack to its fixture'. Almost at once, after laying on down the valley with its familiar series of posts-and-rails, one of the thrusters, Edwardes, elected to put his horse at a gate which lost two bars and put Edwardes 'artistically on his back . . . an expensive amusement with the Drag, as it costs a sovereign'. Despite its loss of two bars, the gate managed to unhorse Willoughby too, while after negotiating a regular steeplechase fence erected by the sportsmen of Chalfont, during the final leg to Gerard's Cross, Hamilton collided with an apple tree, and declared that 'if the tree has half as bad a head ache as he has, it will certainly have no apples this year'.

When we come to 1896 we find an interesting entry for 31 October which is designated as 'the opening day of the so-called legitimate season for the hunting of the drag'. After luncheon at Victoria Barracks, the Master laid on five couple from Datchet Pump just after 3 p.m., and notably to the fore soon afterwards was 'Miss Broom on her good grey . . . revelling in the four big water-jumps' and she 'remained undefeated to the check, finishing over a high and hog-backed gate, a lead which F. V. Gooch alone followed on a little clinker – he was going in his best form all day'. I remember well in my own day with the Staff College Drag how gallantly some of the young ladies rode and I was more than once overtaken by Miss Gott riding a big bay animal which was pulling like the mischief. At the next meet, on 4 November, our correspondent was not out, so he relied on the first whip to supply an account of the day. The two principal items of news were first that the second whip had had a hard time of it summarised thus: 'Second Whip thrown out by a fall – making up leeway – large brook – refusal – dismount – footbridge – lead over anxious horse – trod on his master's toes – ungrateful devil. Advice – Jam him into the brook next time.' The other noteworthy incident was the jumping-upon of Dodd, who, having failed to discover the actual offender, had to satisfy himself by at first breathing general threats, and then, as a mere ensign made bold by his irate state, accosting an innocent and genial field officer with the accusing and awful words: 'Did *you* jump on me?'

It was not only the *Household Brigade Journal* that would report these days out drag-hunting. Even The *Windsor Gazette* had this to say about a meet for the Harrow line:

> The officers of the Brigade of Guards entertained the field to a champagne luncheon, to which over one hundred did justice previous to the run. A special on the G.W.R. conveyed hounds, horses, and riders to the rendezvous at the Red Lion, Southall. The field included the Master, Fryer, Beauclerk, Goulburn, Loftus, Lloyd-Phillips, Mrs Dummett, Gooch, Miss Broom, Pakenham, McNeill, several officers from Hounslow, and many strangers. The hounds were laid on near the iron bridge, Southall, and ran over Messrs Bishop's and Smith's land to Perkins', where they checked. The second line was over Whittington's to Wicklow. The going was heavy, which caused many spills. In the second part of the run the Master had a bad fall, but after pulling himself together, he pluckily remounted and rode to the finish. Mrs Dummett, closely followed by Lieutenants Fryer and Beauclerk, came first in at the finish. The two latter rode wonderfully well to hounds throughout the line.

As we approach the end of the nineteenth century, we find another example of what all hunt servants of military packs of draghounds have no doubt had to contend with – ill-discipline among the hounds. It is not hard to understand why this occurs. Draghounds become notoriously wild if it is the case that the master and his whips are constantly changing, and change of this sort is inevitable because of the constant posting away and posting in of the officers who undertake hunt servants' duties. And all too often the hounds themselves become familiar with particular lines and know where they are going before the master has laid them on. On 23 December the Household Brigade Draghounds met at Sefton Lawn, and because of Windsor races the meet was at 11 o'clock. The former Master, Cholmeley, had resigned and the newly appointed one, Trotter, had an unavoidable duty, so Seymour took on the duties for the day, aided by two wholly inexperienced whips, who afforded the field much amusement by their frantic efforts to keep the hounds under some sort of control at the meet. Nevertheless, they were laid on half an hour later in Mr Gooch's field, and everyone got away over some easy flying fences, although Seymour found himself left behind by going too far left and jumping his horse into a lane from which it was not simple to get out again. He caught up at the check, and then with only a few of the field, as the others, rather surprisingly, had had enough, he completed the second line with the aid of a lead, over some post-and-rails on Mr Van de Weyer's land, given by Fox-Pitt when the Master's and whips' horses refused. It was counted a good line, though shorter than was customary.

The first meet of the new century, on 3 January 1900, was at Beaconsfield and despite heavy rain and a small field there was one feature of the line which highlights the difference between then and now, for 'the going was good and the line easy, all the fences being good flying ones, jumpable anywhere'. Seymour, established as Master now, had an unsuccessful argument with a farmyard gate, which delayed his completion of the first leg, and although the second part of the line also provided the field with a fast run over relatively easy fences, a brook with a hurdle in front produced a boggy landing for Fox-Pitt. A week later, frost having prevented anything earlier, the Drag met at Hayes, but the going was very heavy on the first line, and 'only four out of the field finished, every one's horse being dead-beat. Seymour parted company with his horse at the earliest opportunity he could find, and Foster was seen chasing the famous Dolores round a large grass ride and furrow.' We now find another example of what could occur in the year 1900 out drag-hunting, but not in the year 2000. Very few of the field rode the second line 'all with one horse being obliged to go home'. During my time with the Staff College Drag – and this was nearly 40 years ago – I never came across a member of the field with a second horse. It was a pity that not more of those at the Hayes meet had one, however, for the going was much better from Ickenham to Hayes and was a beautiful bit of country to ride over. Brooke emphasised the relevance of his name by proving 'himself to be a marvellous acrobat, his horse jumping into a brook and he himself landing on the far side. Matters were then rather complicated by his horse scrambling out on the wrong side.'

Most days out drag-hunting can be relied upon to produce a few diverting incidents, and the Sefton Lawn meet on 24 January 1900 certainly turned up trumps, for on the way to the meet one lady driving a dog-cart 'caused a slight disagreement between a prominent member of the Hunt and his horse, the former arriving at the meet with a coat which rather gave one the impression that the matter hadn't ended quite satisfactorily'. But there were compensations, for Mr Gooch entertained the field with his customary hospitality, and even though, as Seymour moved off to lay hounds on at the back of the house, the hounds took affairs into their own control and made off up a lane without orders, they picked up the scent in an orchard and everyone completed the first line well up. The same could not be said of the second line, however, for there were numerous falls, largely because of heavy going. But as the report reads: 'not even the most charitably-minded person could have found excuses for some of them'. The Master himself treated the onlookers to an agreeable spectacle by coming 'off at the last fence, finishing gracefully in full view of every one up at the finish, on his hands and knees'. But as all those who have been fortunate enough to hold the position of MDH would agree with me, the honour, excitement and fun of it infinitely outweigh the occasional misfortunes.

It is good to record that in December 1900 the Household Brigade Drag Hunt entertained the farmers of the Harrow country at luncheon at the King's Head. All the proper toasts – The Queen, Hunt Members, the Farmers – were suitably proposed, drunk and responded to. The only drawback was that there was such a thick mist in the country that the hunting itself was in doubt. But fortitude prevailed and it was decided to go. Only the first line was run as the mist thickened, and a somewhat disappointing day saw the hounds taken back to Windsor by a special from Southall.

At the end of the last chapter I referred to the great interest shown in drag-hunting by the present Prince of Wales's great uncle, and here is part of an account written by the then Master of the Household Brigade Drag Hounds, Captain Sir George Duckworth-King, Bart., which recorded that on Wednesday 1 November 1922, HRH The Prince of Wales honoured the Drag with his presence at luncheon and by riding the lines.

The luncheon was held at Victoria Barracks, Windsor, and was attended by one hundred and twenty landowners, farmers, and members of the Household Brigade Drag Hounds. The health of His Royal Highness was proposed by Lieut.-Col. Lord Henry Seymour, commanding the 3rd Bn. Grenadier Guards, now stationed at Windsor, who, speaking in the name of all present, expressed the very real honour, pride, and gratification that was felt by them at the presence of His Royal Highness that day. The health of His Royal Highness

HRH The Prince of Wales, Windsor 1922 with members, Household Brigade Drag Hunt

having been drunk with acclamation, His Royal Highness very graciously replied to the toast, wishing the Household Brigade Drag Hounds all possible prosperity, both for the present and future seasons. He further pointed out that for all their pleasure and sport followers of the Household Brigade Drag Hounds were indebted to the farmers and landowners over whose ground they rode; and that he himself hoped to ride many lines with the Household Brigade Drag Hounds during the coming season.

After Mr Perkins, himself a former master of draghounds, had proposed the toast of the Drag and expressed his delight that the hounds would be hunting over his land, a sentiment shared by all like him, the Master replied and emphasised his determination to get all damage to fences

83

repaired rapidly. Then Mr Barrett, on behalf of the farmers, stressed what a great source of strength hunting was 'since the same qualities that made a man go well to hounds enabled him to be of use to his country in war or other time of emergency, these qualities being zeal, decision, and determination'. Next came the meet itself at Sefton Lawn at 2.30 p.m. A lot of people and many cameras were there to see the hounds laid on, getting away at a great pace with a field of 'a liberal half-hundred' following.

> The first obstacle was a plain ditch, followed by some three well-grown natural fences, one of which had a considerable drop on the landing side. The line then turned left-handed, providing a double across the lane near the Nag's Head, thence running straight for another two and three-quarter miles across an excellent stretch of country with plenty of fences, most of these having ditches either on the take-off or landing sides. After this distance, the Braywood Inn, bordering the Fifield Road, appeared on the right front, and, the well-known ditch having been negotiated, the check was reached. Time, 12½ minutes; and distance, 3¼ miles.

> A quarter of an hour was spent at the check, and then the hounds were laid on the second line. Scent was perfect, and the pack went away at a tremendous pace; and the country not being so cramped as in the first line, while the fences were jumpable almost anywhere; the field had a really fine gallop, the pace of the run throughout approaching that of a fast point-to-point race. There were a good many casualties in the second line, but fortunately no one was hurt; still, by the time Geys House, Holyport, was reached, the field had been considerably thinned out, not more than some thirty finishing, whereas some fifty riders had been present at the meet. The hounds finished well together, and seemed fresh enough to have gone a third line, had they been asked to do so. The distance was about the same as the first line, but the time was faster, being eleven minutes. Thus, although the weather was against us, being both cold and wet, the opening meet was considered by all to have provided a thoroughly good afternoon's sport.

Those of us who have enjoyed and are still enjoying drag-hunting will agree wholeheartedly. How we would have liked to have ridden the lines with the Household Brigade Draghounds that day! Here we will bid them *adieu* but not before adding that in my day with the Staff College Drag we hunted a line very similar to theirs, and indeed I believe it is still in use. Although the Staff College and Sandhurst Draghounds now constitute the only military pack that I know of, there have been many others in the past, among them our own 4th Hussars pack in Italy and Germany, the Wessex Hounds established by the Queen's Bays and showing great sport in the country between Celle and Verden, and most notably the Royal Artillery (Woolwich) Draghounds.

5

The Royal Artillery Drag

'There is a word you often see, pronounce it as you may –
"You bike", "you bykwe", "ubbikwe" – alludin' to R.A.
It serves 'Orse, Field, an' Garrison as motto for a crest,
An' when you've found out all it means, I'll tell you 'alf the rest.'

Kipling

Royal Artillery (Woolwich) Drag in the Weald of Kent

As far as hunting goes, the Royal Artillery certainly lived up to their motto *Ubique*, for at one time or another they had packs of hounds at Woolwich, Salisbury Plain, Bordon, Dover, Troon and Oswestry. Three of them were of draghounds – Woolwich, Bordon and Oswestry – three were of beagles – Dover, Troon and Larkhill – one, Salisbury Plain, originally harriers, and later for fox-hunting. Only this last one now survives. The RA (Woolwich) Drag was founded by Captain A. H. W. Williams RA in 1866, the first master being a veterinary surgeon, W. Thacker, and the drag-lines were laid in the country near Woolwich and Eltham. It was very popular, not only with the Gunners themselves, but with many of the local community too. In 1879 the pack suffered from an outbreak of rabies and had to be destroyed, and although a new pack was established for the 1882–83 season, a year later there was another outbreak of rabies and again the pack was destroyed. But the Drag started up yet again and flourished.

The Boer War brought yet one more interruption in drag-hunting, but there was such enthusiasm and support for the pack that it was again re-started in October 1900. As with other military packs of draghounds, war continued to interrupt – this time the Great War 1914–18 – yet the Woolwich Drag was reformed in time for the 1918–19 season. Because the surrounding country had become so much built over, lines were laid further away, as far as Sevenoaks and Edenbridge in Kent and Romford and Upminster in Essex. During the 1920s and 1930s the Woolwich Drag was very popular, but mechanisation of the Royal Artillery had its effect. No longer were so many fifteen-bobbers available[1] and the knell was finally sounded at the approach of the Second World War. In mid-1939 not only did the Woolwich Drag come to an end, but so too did the Royal Artillery (Bordon) Drag, which had been established in 1923–24 with drag-lines in the country of the HH, Hambledon and Chiddingfold Hunts. Even this, however, was not the end of the Royal Artillery's championing of drag-hunting, for in 1950 the Oswestry Drag was formed by Brigadier Peter Gregson and Jasper Browell to carry on the traditions which had been so notably successful at Woolwich. Five couple of hounds had been drafted from the North Shropshire Hunt, and drag-lines were laid within a 5-mile radius of Oswestry in country on loan from the Tanatside, North Shropshire and Sir W. William-Wynn's Hunts. Peter Gregson and Major Edmeades were Joint Masters, and the Oswestry Drag survived until the 1956–57 season.

But the Royal Artillery are to be congratulated for all that they still do for the equestrian world. Racing at Larkhill is immensely popular and excellently run. Also, at Larkhill in October every year, there is a hunter trial for many different classes, and it is always good to see that on these occasions there are many military contestants – from the King's Troop, the Household Cavalry and the Royal Navy. Above all the Royal Artillery (Salisbury Plain) Hunt still thrives – it was in 1946 that the Hunt was

[1] Troop horses, hired for hunting or other private use, were known as 'fifteen-bobbers', this being the modest monthly charge.

officially recognised by the MFH Association, although it had originated as far back as 1907 as a harrier pack with kennels at Bulford. Today, as the only remaining regimental pack of foxhounds in the British Army, it has country on permanent loan from the South and West Wilts and the Tedworth Hunts, bounded by West Lavington, Wylye, Salisbury, Andover, Bulford and Rushall, with access to Imber and Bulford training areas. The Hunt's own point-to-point is always held at Larkhill, as too are the point-to-points of many adjacent hunts. Their distinctive uniform is a green coat with a scarlet collar.

The illustrations of the RA Woolwich Drag which appear here are, of course, by Gilbert Holiday, of whom his great contemporary, Lionel Edwards, wrote: 'No one can, or ever could, depict the horse in motion better than Gilbert did.' It was while out with the Woolwich Drag, whose activities he recorded so vividly and accurately, that Gilbert broke his back in an accident in 1933, but despite this tragedy he went on painting as brilliantly as ever, giving to the world a wonderful example of pluck and cheerfulness. He loved horses and was extremely bold riding to hounds. As one of his Gunner friends wrote in an obituary, the lines which accompanied a picture of his portrayed absolutely the artist himself:

When the going is deep and the hedges are blind,
May you ne'er lack a friend who will stop and be kind.

Whether depicting a point-to-point, the Grand National, the huntsman in action with his hounds, a meet or hacking home, Gilbert Holiday was 'perhaps the greatest action painter of the horse in the history of equestrian art'. The days he had with the Woolwich Drag certainly produced many incidents worthy of his skill, and we are fortunate that the records of this Hunt are both numerous and detailed.

For the 1926–27 season they had no fewer than nineteen different lines, some as far as 17 miles from the RA Mess, some as close as 4 miles. There would be fields of up to 75 with many locals riding, and the records would show that on 21 March 1927, for the last line of that season, the going was perfect and hounds ran well. A few seasons later we find an entry for November 1929:

Hounds met at Court Lodge, Brasted instead of Mottingham in perfect weather. 15 couple on. Field of 55. Some horses trained from Chislehurst to Sevenoaks. Laid on at foot of Westerham Hill, black and tans ran riot into Westerham Wood and only rejoined pack at Force Green check. Then past

A Fifteen-Bobber being snobbish

Court Lodge to finish at Clevening Halt. Hounds ran beautifully and going good. Fair number of falls, none serious. Will Freeman (from Grafton), huntsman to W. Kent remarked how well hounds hunted on a wide head with a good cry from start to finish. The pack has been improved by the removal of the fast mute hounds and this season they are run on a lighter scent. Mr Dark entertained the field to tea. 6 miles.

From so brief and factual a summary all of us who have enjoyed drag-hunting can picture what has been left out – the anticipatory chat at the meet, greeting old friends, hacking to where hounds are laid on, surge to the first fence, joy at not being one of the fallers, tightening of girths at the check, and exhilaration at finishing well. Things did not always go so smoothly, as a meet at Upminster two weeks later showed.

On this day, a wild and stormy one, the number of hounds out, eleven and a half couple, exceeded the field of fifteen which included the hunt servants. Of these, nine fell at the second fence, a flooded brook, and there was then a long delay at the first check while those members of the field who had dismounted without permission rounded up their loose horses. This took so long that when hounds were laid on the second part of the line, they were a full hour behind the runner, and the consequent weakening of the scent made it necessary for the Master, as it were, to show hounds the way. They rallied at the end, however – trust them to do so – and hunted on to the worry in a bunch. Despite these mishaps, the line was pronounced to be a splendid one which rode light except for the first few fields.

It was not only in their own accounts of their days' drag-hunting that these activities were so lovingly and graphically recorded. An article in *Grays and Tilbury Gazette* of 25 January 1930 not only told its readers about the events of two days before, but sought also to educate these same readers about the ins-and-outs of drag-hunting. It is very well done.

The only living creatures who were concerned with 'worry' of any form at a meet of the R.A. (Woolwich) Draghounds, at Cranham, on Thursday, were the hounds, and they disposed of it with considerable promptitude. 'Worry', of course, is the term applied to the flesh that awaits them at the finish of the drag and where the scent ends. This, then, was the only aspect in which worry figured in the chase, for it proved to be most enjoyable, and none the less exhilarating because it was stiff.

It is the practice of these riders to meet alternately in Essex and Kent, but they have been rather unlucky recently in regard to the weather when the line has been selected in this county. Two meets for the Harold Wood and Brentwood districts had to be cancelled at the last moment, but this, the most recent, made amends.

About fifty riders with fourteen couple of hounds assembled at the Thatched House, Cranham, where Mr G. Barton was host, at about two o'clock, the hounds having been brought down by van from the Charlton Kennels. There was a large number of interested onlookers present when Mr R. McKeller, one of the best runners at the garrison, set off five minutes after the hour to lay the scent with a sack containing fox litter. The line was mapped out by Mr Manning of Ockenden and covered a distance of about seven miles. The runner was given about a quarter of an hour's start of hounds, and he made off at a fast pace across Pike Lane towards Mr Fisher's farm by way of the fields. He was soon lost to sight of the watchers, but it was possible to discern the heads of the riders for a longer period when they set off later. The field made a fine sight once the hounds had laid hold of the scent, but it was not long before two falls were reported.

Three checks were made, the first being at Mr Knight's farm, North Ockenden; the next at Corner Farm, Bulvan, and the third at Puddledock Wood, about a mile from the finish. The two biggest ditches were within the last mile and a half, the water at the second being several feet deep. Here many of the riders had difficulty in getting the horses to take it, but there were no mishaps. Mrs Revell Smith, wife of the Master, riding side saddle, had a particularly shy animal, but she refused to be beaten and, having negotiated the ditch, laughingly called out an apology to a photographer standing by in readiness for a fall.

Perhaps the most interesting feature at the finish was to notice how the hounds quickened their pace to pounce in a growling mass on to the 'worry'. Within three minutes nearly half a hundred-weight of flesh had disappeared. The runner returned half an hour before the field, but he is not always so lucky. He has been overtaken by the dogs and, not unnaturally on those occasions, he drops the litter to enable him to get away. Foxhounds, however, will not maul human beings and he does not run any serious risk of injury.

'It has been a most enjoyable run,' said the Master, Captain Revell Smith, at the conclusion. 'The going was a bit heavy and there were several big jumps, but they were taken well and there have not been as many falls as usual. We should like very sincerely to thank the local farmers for their courtesy and also for their hospitality. It has been one of our most pleasant runs from all points of view.'

Which of us, who has had the honour and joy of being master of a pack of draghounds, would not have been pleased to read such an account of one of our own days with the drag? Another newspaper cutting, this one showing a photograph of a meet at Woolwich Garrison itself, bears the delightful caption 'We're Thirsty, Too' – and depicts hounds clustered round the mess sergeant and one of his staff, beautifully turned out in livery and about to dispense stirrup cups to those present. It is clear that the hounds are making first bid for whatever stimulant is being offered.

In examining the admirable records of the Royal Artillery Drag from 1926 to 1934, many other treasures are revealed – a notice of the hunter and hound trial of the South Oxon Farmers' Draghounds, held at Chazey Farm, Mapledurham on Wednesday 22 October 1930, figures prominently among them. It must have been quite a day. There were five classes of hunter trial events, including one reserved for subscribers and farmers of the South Oxon Drag, a ladies' open, heavy and lightweight open events, an inter-hunt team class; *and* taking us right back to Peter Beckford's times, a hound trial, open to all, with the first prize of a cup and £2-0-0 'to the hound completing the course, over which a Fox Drag will be laid, in the shortest time'. Here was the re-enactment of what Lin Jenkins had written about the origin of trail scents 'as foxhound contests which could be easily watched as one hunt pitted their prowess against another'. The RA Drag had reason to remember this day for they walked off with most of the cups. The ladies' open class was won by the sporting Mrs Revell Smith's Watty; they won the inter-hunt team event *and* were equal second; they won the heavyweight open; and one of their hounds, Manager, was first in the hound trial.

A similar sort of day was run by the Royal Engineers' Drag Hunt Club on – of all days – Friday 13 March 1931, and what is so noteworthy about these events is the beautifully produced official programmes and plans of the course. For the hound trial six packs of draghounds were entered:

Tring Farmers Drag, one couple; Household Brigade Drag, two couples; Mid-Surrey Drag, two couples; Shorncliffe Garrison Drag, one couple; Royal Artillery Drag, two couples; Royal Engineers Drag, two couples. The first prize for the hound 'completing the course, over which a fox drag will be laid, in the shortest time' had been presented by J. E. C. McCandlish Esq, RE MDH; it would be handed over by Mrs Pritchard, wife of Major-General Pritchard, by whose kind permission the band of the Royal Engineers would play during the afternoon. Things were done properly in those wonderful days when the horse still played so prominent a part in the life of the British Army. Every year the Royal Artillery Drag ran their point-to-point. Every year they had their hunt ball, and one of Gilbert Holiday's less well known, but endearing drawings appears on the dance programme for the 1934 ball – it shows a good-looking, saddled and bridled horse gazing benevolently down upon a hound turning his head up to return the message of affection, and underneath appear the words: 'Invitation to the Waltz'. Another of Gilbert Holiday's wonderful drawings is featured on the menu for the RA Draghunt's Farmers' Dinner, held in the Woolwich Mess on 15 November 1935. We are all familiar with the Johnny Walker whisky advertisement. Gilbert Holiday gives us a member of the Hunt, beautifully mounted in immaculate hunting kit with hunting topper and monocle – a self portrait? – and beside him the words 'Born 1866'. Below is drawn a horse-trailer being pulled by a car, and beneath is the twin caption: 'Still going strong'.

There is an agreeable entry in the Royal Engineers' hunter and hound trials programme for 1934, which introduces a special prize of the Mounted Infantry Cup – to be awarded to the best performance in either the subscribers' or open event by an officer member of the RE Drag Hunt Club, riding a troop or draft horse. The programme also stipulated that those eligible *might* enter for more than one event, but could only *do* one round, which would count for any of three events, so that no horse could gain from having done a previous round, a stipulation that was almost certainly welcome to the horses themselves.

The Woolwich Drag hunting journal for the 1935–36 season is a model of how such things should be done. Each day is fully described, with details of hounds, hunt staff, how the day went and very often a sketch map of the line. It would perhaps weary the reader to be presented with too many accounts of the season's hunting, but the writer's summary is so

Royal Artillery (Woolwich) Drag

relevant to our story that it deserves attention. Having noted how many lines and which ones were hunted, together with names of hounds and the hunt staff, he goes on to discuss how the Master and his staff succeeded in making hounds steadier and making a day's drag-hunting more realistic.

Hounds were rather unsteady at the beginning of the season and a lot of riot had been experienced in previous years. Regent was on the lookout for trouble and had to be 'corrected' once or twice. As the confidence of the staff improved, so the pack became steadier, and by half way through the season, it was normal for two Whips to take hounds out on exercise through the streets of Woolwich on their own. I'm sure the secret of this was coolness and quietness on the part of the Staff in the presence of possible riot, such as stray dogs and cats, and the instant correction of any hound who even looked at them. A lot of shouting and whip cracking the moment a stray dog appears only excites the pack and draws their attention to the trouble . . . The Master's policy throughout the season has been to run the Drag as realistically as possible. Instead of running a small number of hounds on a red hot scent, between 14 to 18 couple of hounds were taken out, and they were made to puzzle out the lines for themselves. Instead of being held up at checks, hounds were allowed to try and work it out on their own, and then if they failed, they were cast by the Master in such a manner as to bring them across the line. If possible the lay-on was made as realistic as possible, i.e. hounds were made to draw a covert . . . Further, hounds instead of running right in front of the field and being constantly jumped on and hustled, were kept to one flank or the other.

This admirable summing up goes on to point out that it was no easy task to teach hounds, who hitherto had been following a powerful drag scent, suddenly to hunt and draw properly; indeed there was a great deal of doubt as to whether it could be done at all. But here was one more instance that perseverance keeps honour bright, and as the season advanced hounds became steadier, the whips better at controlling them, and of course the conduct of affairs, however innovative, was more interesting for all concerned. In making his report the writer does not overlook the all important matter of keeping landowners and farmers content to welcome the drag on their land. This, he properly maintains, is the business of line secretaries, who must visit *every* farmer and landowner on their line at least once before and once after each occasion that the drag runs over their land. This comprehensive report lists all the line secretaries for the seventeen lines of the Hunt, and gives a short, vivid pen-picture of each line, including where the meet is, its distance from Woolwich, what it is like, how to get there, whether second horses are needed and if so where. There is also a complete catalogue of hounds and bitches with the number of days they hunted. In short the whole thing is a piece of work which could not be bettered. Beautifully written, both in its script and choice of language, so that the scenes and action it portrays come alive when read by a new eye more than 60 years after its composition, detailed, painstaking and lovingly produced, to my mind it stands up peerless, and demonstrates what a superlative drag hunt was run by the Royal Artillery at Woolwich to inspire such a history of its 1935–36 season. The Hunt was fortunate indeed to have the services of the same scribe for the following season, and we may perhaps be permitted to include his report of a day in November 1936, when the hounds met at 2 p.m. at Captain Kyffen's house, with a field of 30-odd, weather fine, but going rather wet; the runner had left at 1.15.

Hounds moved off at 2.10 and were quickly on to the line in a field alongside the drive. They ran on at a good pace parallel to the Rly line till they reached a road which they crossed. Then turning right handed they crossed the Upminster road at a sharp corner and ran almost due east over some good big ditches and post and rails. Hounds were at fault just short of the road near Mrs Hoare's Fur and were cast across the road, hitting it off along the edge of a drive leading to Field House. Turning slightly left they hunted well to E. Horndon Station, where they were picked up and taken over the Rly bridge by the Station. They were cast left handed round a field beyond the Station, and hitting off the line on the right they headed for the Southend road, turning left they ran parallel to the road past Nutty's Fm for about ½mile and then threw up. Second horses were met here and hounds were lifted over the main road and almost immediately owned the line on the far side and headed for Jury Hill. Turning left hounds ran up past Mr Bloomfield's Fm, whom we were all delighted to see cheering us on with his customary enthusiasm.

The going was a good deal heavier now and there was a lot of grief. Hounds ran on past Childeditch Hall and on up towards Warley Lodge, throwing up on some waste ground by a X-roads. Hounds were then taken through a farmyard and owned the line in a field beyond . . . A very enjoyable line which was greatly improved by recent additions. The field was greatly reduced by a lot of grief – there are some good solid fences and plenty of room – and only two or three besides the staff finished the line. Hounds hunted well and were all on with the exception of Pastime at the worry. They were still tailed off at times and are not yet fit. They hunted with plenty of music, Whimper didn't try at all.

No doubt Pastime and Whimper were later required to give their reasons in writing for not performing better. There were now only two more seasons before, as one report put it, 'hunting was to be interfered with by the European crisis', and we may perhaps take a brief look at both of them.

A meet at Penshurst on 1 November 1937 with a field of 34, including twelve gentlemen cadets, wet weather and heavy going, did not exactly go according to plan. The runner had moved off at 1 p.m., and the hounds, having been unboxed at the meet, drew their first covert near Ford Place at 2.15. They were quickly on to the line and there was a good half mile of wide fences for the field until the first check. Then after another mile or so parallel to the Medway and through a hop field, they checked again. It was then that the hounds elected to make their own decisions. After laying on again, only three couple, including Coxcomb, Preacher and Pagan, went away on the line, while the remainder, eleven and a half couple, hunted a heel line, but rejoined later when the leaders threw up on the slopes of Star Hill, where second horses were waiting. The next part of the line, from the hill across a wooded valley to another, went well although Bangle and Helen were a long way behind. But in the wood itself again the pack split, only three

Royal Artillery (Woolwich) Drag

97

and a half couple going away on the line, others hunting some selected scent of their own, and only rejoining about fifteen minutes after the leaders had reached the worry. Yet in spite of these departures from the actual plan of campaign, despite even the heavy going and the rain, both military and civilian participants greatly enjoyed the day and pronounced the line to be a success. In his report the Secretary noted that he very nearly realised his great ambition of completing a line without falling off – only to misjudge the last fence!

Later in that season the hounds were confronted with the confusing problem of encountering a fox. After meeting at Franks Farm early in January 1938, and having completed the first part of the line at a great pace with plenty of big ditches and post-and-rail fences, they checked near East Horndon Station and, after being lifted over the railway and laid on again, 'at the first fence, a fox got up about 10 yards ahead of the leaders. He was hunted in a left handed circle, and made for some farm buildings, where hounds were successfully whipped off'. Nor was this the only distraction, for as hounds continued to hunt the line they found another fox in Codham Hall wood, and this time, because of thick undergrowth, it took the whips much longer to get hounds back on the line which led back to Franks Farm. By the time the leaders got to the worry – with Prussian, who did not always perform so well, still very much to the fore – hounds were well strung out. It seems that, as an experiment, the runner started laying the scent at the finish, running the line backwards, having moved off nearly one and three-quarter hours before hounds hacked away from the meet. Hounds were laid on heel as soon as the runner got in, the idea being to simulate the strong scent of a fresh fox and the fading scent of a tired one. The effect, of course, was that the hounds hunted the first 3 miles of the line at a really fast pace, and later were so strung out. It was ironical that on this very day M. Renard should have put in an appearance not once, but twice.

The last meet of the 1937–38 season was on 21 March, when with excellent going and fine, warm weather, a field of about twenty and thirteen couple of hounds enjoyed a good, fast run with some splendid fences, and all the hounds, except Heedless who lived up to her name by being late on parade, were on at the worry. This was the last line for the then Master and first whip, both of whom were leaving Woolwich, and was 'an extremely pleasing and happy finish to the season'.

The new master for the 1938–39 season was Captain E. H. Colville RA.[2] There were several puppy lines before the opening meet on 17 October, and at one of them there was another unplanned encounter with foxes. This, of course, was the time when the Munich Agreement about Czechoslovakia had averted, or perhaps we should say postponed, war and had given rise to the comment that Europe's crisis had not yet interfered with drag-hunting. On this occasion the meet was at Eynsford on a perfect autumn day, and although the going was firm there was plenty of good old turf. Having hacked off from the meet punctually at 2.30 p.m., hounds found the line near Range Valley and

> . . . ran at a good pace along the side of the valley in which rabbit holes caused the field some anxiety. Turning up the hill they checked in a large field near Dunstall Farm and, a wide cast having proved fruitless, they were taken on to Highfield Wood in which a brace of foxes were soon afoot. The Master saw one and Eden another, also one of the field saw *the biggest wot ever was seen.*

The pack was turned and soon had the line of the drag once more, going on to the finish at Upper Austin Lodge. Comments on the hounds' performance were varied. Pagan had been hanging back during the latter part of the run; Rampant, Worker and Reckless were not up at the worry. Verer was promising and had hunted well. Breaker seemed keen to learn.

The Master, Captain Colville, noted after a subsequent puppy line that a number of uninvited civilians had not behaved properly, but had abused the hospitality of the farmers by riding where they chose. The culprits seemed to be members of the various riding schools in Kent, and the Master decreed that they were a nuisance and only those invited should be allowed to come out in future. Captain Colville would quite frequently add his own comments to the Secretary's account of a day's hunting, and noted after a November meet that, with the exception of two and a half couple, hounds had gone well in the Orsett country, and that 'three bits of open water in quick succession gave the field [some twenty were out that day] something to think about'. As for the erring hounds, they ran heel

[2] Damer Colville, his son, was one of my whips during my time with the Staff College Drag. He has most generously let me see the diaries and records of both the RA Woolwich Drag and the RA Bordon Drag. His uncle, J. D. C. Ellison, was Joint Master of the Bordon Drag. These sources have been invaluable.

back to the start, then forward again to the Fen – 'three times over the same line, before they could be got under control! A good lesson for the Whips.'

It is pleasing to record that the Woolwich Drag sent a team over to take part in the hunter trials of the Mid-Surrey Drag – still going strong – which was held in late October at Highfield Farm, Epsom. The Royal Artillery came fourth, all three places ahead of them having been taken by the Mid-Surrey themselves. The success of the Farmers' Dinner on 28 November 1938 may be judged by recording that it began at 7 p.m. and the last guest was seen off at 4 a.m. next morning. The Hunt also had a splendid Christmas card for that year, in which Snaffles depicts what appear to be the Major and the Memsahib doing the 'Woolwich Trot', that is, having dismounted involuntarily, trotting after their horses which are about to jump a hedge at the far end of the field in the company of several other horses and riders, one of whom is clearly about to part company with his four-legged friend.

Royal Artillery (Woolwich) Draghounds

This last season before the war – and, alas, the last of all – had been very successful, with no fewer than 39 days' drag hunting. The two last meets were in March 1939 at Orsett and Ash, and of these the former was the better one for all went well, with hounds running at a good pace over excellent country. We may note here too that it was the last season for Tom Homewood, Senior Bombadier Royal Horse Artillery, who had been kennel-huntsman to the Woolwich Drag for so long and retired only when the Drag itself ceased to exist. 'Tom was a wonderful man,' wrote Colville in a tribute which appeared in *The Gunner*, January 1976,

> . . . always cheerful, delighted to see old friends of whom he had many, and a valued companion and guide to Masters and Whips who changed every three years or so. Tom was the heart and soul of the Drag and many a Gunner, as well as a host of other people had days of fun through him. The Royal Regiment owes a debt it can never repay to one of its most loyal and devoted servants.

Tom Homewood died in 1975 within a few days of his ninety-fourth birthday. It is to such men, as well as to horse and hound, that we owe the best of our fun.

During that last memorable season the Woolwich Drag had also sent two teams to take part in hunter trials organised by the RA Bordon Drag, and we must now say something about them. There are several accounts of the Bordon Drag's origins, and one of them was written in 1938 by Colonel C. E. Vickery, CMG, DSO, DL, JP, then Chairman of Durham County Council, in the form of a letter to J. Ellison, then serving in the Royal Artillery at Bordon. Colonel Vickery explains that the Drag was started in 1923–24 by Guille, a subaltern in the Royal Artillery, and assisted by two others, Lieutenants Bedford and Yates, each of whom contributed £5 towards the purchase of hounds, as well as obtaining 'gift' hounds. It was really a revival of the former Longmoor Mounted Infantry Drag which had been established after the Boer War. Another source reveals that at first there were no kennels, but hounds were 'trencher' fed as in olden days by other officers of the two brigades stationed at Bordon, and on a hunting day the hounds would be brought or sent to the meet by their 'owners'. At the meet itself everyone taking part was capped sixpence (2½p today) towards expenses such as paying the runner, mending fences and so on. It was clearly a fairly amateurish arrangement at the time. The early masters were Bedford, Guille and Swinton Lee, then in September 1926 Vickery took on the mastership for the next two seasons.

In his letter to Ellison, who became Joint Master in 1938, Vickery goes on to say that they had some trouble with Aldershot where those running their Drag were concerned that the Bordon Hunt had too many of the good lines in that part of the country and wanted to claim some for themselves. But the dispute was sorted out by discussion between the two masters. By Vickery's time the hounds were kept in the sick horses' lines, and they then had sixteen to eighteen couple. The Hunt staff wore hunt hats, black tail coats, cords and black boots. Expenses were kept low and were principally confined to feeding the hounds. Nevertheless, a Bordon Hunt Club was formed with subscriptions from those in the garrison. 'I never understood how the Infantry stuck it,' wrote Vickery, 'for they were the principal subscribers and they came out very seldom because those damned Weedon[3] people always wanted to put up trick fences in a line which of course put out all those who had not school-trained horses.' The Colonel added one point which will ring a bell with many of us who have subsequently made excellent use of national assets, whether human or material, to forward some sporting activity, particularly those concerned with equitation: 'I enlisted a soldier as kennel man, but of course this was not known by the Army Council.'

We have already followed some of the Woolwich Drag's runs in the 1930s. Here are a few, notably concise accounts of what the Bordon Drag got up to in the 1920s. In November 1926 hounds met at The Red Lion, Oakhanger in poorish conditions, yet despite heavy rain, which produced some soft patches here and there on the Greatham line, the going was generally good and a field of 24, starting at Hartley Wood Farm with ten couple and two checks, enjoyed negotiating 33 fences with hounds going extremely well. The report notes that 'a fresh supply of foxwater having been obtained from the Staff College Kennels, Camberley' their old stock could be thrown away.

Just over a year later, in December 1927, six couple of hounds met at Norton Farm on a cold, raw, foggy afternoon for the Hartley Park line and a field of eighteen overcame the rather heavy going on the first half to enjoy an excellent run after the check over the HH point-to-point fences

---

[3] Weedon was the Cavalry School.

where the going was much better. The scent was good, and hounds, after a somewhat uncertain start, ran well.

These cameos of a day's drag-hunting, while lacking the abundance of incident and character which featured in some other accounts we have followed, give the essentials and will have proved most valuable for succeeding hunt staff and line secretaries. There is perhaps room for two more, the first in the New Year of 1928, when eight couple met at East Lodge, East Tisted for the Rotherfield Park line. Some previous meets had been cancelled because of heavy snowfalls and a blizzard, but on this day, 18 January, there was only a slight drizzle with a south-west wind, and it proved an excellent day.

> The usual 4½ miles with 2 checks made up the line. Hounds went exceptionally well, and the field were Thrusters all. The going was very fair. This proved to be quite our best afternoon up to date. The field numbered 28, including two ladies, Miss Standish and Miss Wansborough; they both rode extremely well and were not among the fallen. There were numerous spectators. The Hunt dinner followed. The Royal Sussex band played. The afternoon and evening were great successes.

The last drag-line of the season was also at Rotherfield Park on 21 March, conditions fine, overcast, no wind, seven couple of hounds, and 'owing to a lot of fresh plough on the West side of Winchester this line was slightly shorter than usual but was if anything improved by crossing the Ripley road immediately after the first check. Hounds ran very well indeed, and it was a most successful line. The going was good. Capt. Scott MFH kindly entertained us at his house before we moved off. Field of 22 including one lady.' Pithy, these entries in the Bordon Drag hunting journal certainly are, but very much to the point. How some of us long for such brevity and relevance in many of those who wield their ponderous pens today.

There are, however, times when it is necessary to write at some length in order to trace the origin of this or that, and one such occasion was when Colonel Hammick explained in a letter to the Officer Commanding at Bordon how the Drag there had become a Royal Artillery pack. Until 1931 it had been a station pack of hounds run by Gunner officers, but early in 1932 the then OC Troops had expressed the wish that the Royal Artillery should take it over, and Colonel Hammick, as the senior Artillery officer there, had agreed to provide the necessary support provided the pack became quite clearly a Royal Artillery one. As a result the title was changed and the Gunner hunt coat – dark blue with red collar – was adopted by the Master and hunt servants in place of the former scarlet coats. While this change of status gave the Gunners a free hand in the control of the Hunt, it brought with it, of course, obligations towards both subscribers and farmers. They gladly took upon themselves the privilege of being hosts to the farmers at the annual dinner, the hunter trials and the RA point-to-point. The success of their venture may be gauged by recording that for the 1932–33 season the Hunt's supporters, members and farmers, totalled about *170!* This success is not to be wondered at, for to read the administrative notes and instructions prepared by various masters and secretaries of the Bordon Drag is to see with what immense dedication, conscientiousness, grasp of detail, personal attention to the welfare of those serving the Hunt, and sheer diligence these men set about their duties.

One such set of notes is awesome in its thoughtfulness and thoroughness. Running to 20-odd different headings, with many sub-headings, it deals with payment scales for the staff, their insurance, clothing and fuel supply; a broad programme of events for the season, starting with the Committee meeting in August, fixing puppy lines, printing of invitations, subscriptions, list of meets, printing meet cards, arranging the Farmers' Dinner, alerting all line secretaries, getting Hunt stationery, Drag notice board, liaising with railway companies for drag trams; then capping policy, despatch of meet cards, warning cards for all farmers; hound van, insurance, meal and meat, hound cards; diary to include a meeting for organising the point-to-point, hunter trials; horse trailers for the master and whips; finance and its management. One entry in this particular set of notes deserves quotation:

> Farmers List: This is MOST IMPORTANT. Consists of Index Cards and a book. Essential to keep it up to date, and Line Secretaries can give you great help in this. It is far better to have too many names on this than too few. On the other hand every obsolete name may cost the Drag a good deal p.a. in dinner, lunch and drink. Farmers let us bash their fences and ride their land.

We might add here that the farmers are more than welcome to ride with us, and, of course, we will repair their fences. Another fine example of the careful documentation which characterised the running of the Royal Artillery (Bordon) Hounds is their record of the hounds for the season 1938–39.[4] There were at that time two masters, Captain Blacker and Mr J. Ellison; four whippers-in, Captains Sykes, Smithwick, Scholfield and McLeod; two hon. secretaries, Major Gilkes and Mr Allen; and the all-important kennel-man was Gunner Legge. Kennels were at Oxney Farm, Bordon. Yet not all this care could ensure that there were not occasional comings to grief in the field.

I cannot say that our own regimental pack of draghounds in the 4th Hussars enjoyed quite the same administrative care and excellence of those in the Royal Artillery, for ours was essentially an improvised and short-lived affair, but that we matched them for sheer fun and excitement was never in doubt.

[4] See page 184.

6

The Best of My Fun

'My horses all pull like the mischief and rush like devils and
want a deal of riding . . . I prefer to have something to do on
horseback. When a man tells me that a horse is an armchair, I
always tell him to put the brute into his bedroom.'
Lord Chiltern in *Phineas Finn* by Anthony Trollope

The first horse that I rode with our own regimental pack of draghounds
was certainly no armchair and did pull like the mischief. I had been
told that Partisan, as he was named, would go best in a snaffle, but it was
quite clear at the meet, which was at an old farmhouse in the grass and
stone-wall country north-east of Trieste, that he was going to be a handful,
for no sooner had he seen the hounds and heard the sound of the horn
than, like Phineas Finn's mount, Bonebreaker, he 'stretched out his head,
and put his mouth upon the bit, and began to tremble in every muscle'.
Give him lots of room, I was advised, and like Phineas I reflected that an
insurance office would charge dearly for my life at that moment. Yet to
start with I had every reason to be satisfied with Partisan, for he seemed to

*'Shove him
along at this
one'*

106

have a passion for leaping over stone walls, and by keeping him well clear of the field, we were not giving trouble to others. It was not until the third leg that I felt any desire to change him for an armchair because until then I seemed to be just in control, except when we were in sight of and nearing the next stone wall. But shortly after we had set off on the final leg, Partisan and myself still keeping clear of the field, I heard furious voices behind me and recognised those of a bold-riding and wholly eccentric couple – the Major and his Memsahib of a neighbouring cavalry regiment, respectively known as 'Crash' and 'Wonky' – who seemed to be indulging in a dispute as to whose animal would complete the run first. Wonky was the first to draw level with me, on the nearside, and then Crash on the offside, and they were still yelling imprecations at one another and at their galloping steeds. This commotion was too much for Partisan, and with a bound that almost unseated me, he shot forward with a clearly intense desire to shake off such undesirable fellows of the chase and moreover to ensure that it would be himself and I who finished well ahead of the two of them. Somehow I stayed on board, only to receive a reprimand from the Colonel at the end of the line for not being 'well down in the saddle'. The fact was that it was only by standing up in the stirrups that I was able to stop Partisan from taking me across the so-called Morgan Line, a provisional border with Tito's Yugoslavia, whose frontier guards did not take kindly to trespassing British officers.

But you might well ask at this point – how did it come about that your regiment had a pack of draghounds in such an unlikely place as Venezia Giulia? In explaining this circumstance I must go back a few months. The scene – the 4th Hussars' barracks at Villa Opicina – the time – September 1945. As I strolled towards the stables to see how my handsome bay gelding, Hungry, was getting on the Regimental Orderly Corporal appeared in my path. Immaculate in shirt-sleeve order with cross-belt superbly blancoed, boots like glass and cap-badge gleaming, he saluted, eyes tilted skywards as if regarding heaven, and spoke. They were words he had used a hundred times to many different members of the regiment: 'The Commanding Officer's compliments, Sir, and could you spare him a few moments?' In other words, the Colonel is in an implacable rage about something, is tolerably certain that you are the culprit and wishes instantly, or at any rate as soon as you can reach his office, to break every bone in your body, strip you of all regimental accoutrements and despatch you to be OC Troops, Mogadishu, never to be seen or heard of again.

I have always admired one officer of ours who, having received a comparable summons, did the unthinkable and simply failed to appear. When, at luncheon in the mess, the adjutant demanded to know why he had not come when sent for, he returned the devastating answer: 'I was too busy'. The unparalleled impudence of this reply is only properly understood when I say that he was the idlest, most useless, yet none the less charming young man that the regiment had ever been saddled with. No such initiative presented itself to me as I scurried across the square toward the orderly room. I was far too busy going over in my mind the activities of the last week or so in order to identify the particular misdemeanor for which I was clearly about to be arraigned and to have some sort of explanation to hand. The trouble was that there was such a wide selection to choose from. This state of affairs sprang from our naturally high spirits as we got down to that frequently sighed-for process, sighed for that is while the war was still on, of 'getting back to real soldiering'. This phrase, often employed by the pre-war members of the regiment, referred to the abandonment of such things as training, parades, work of any sort really, and instead a concentration on the more agreeable pastimes of sport, travel, good food and wine, parties and mixing more with the female of the species. So that for wartime officers like myself, who had recently passed the necessary boards and been properly gazetted to the 4th Hussars, this return to proper soldiering came as a very agreeable surprise.

It was true that certain disciplinary regulations had been tightened, that more attention to dress and smartness, regimental customs and formalities, like the trumpeters sounding 'stables' at 11 o'clock, formal dining in mess and so on had been revived. It was true that the Regimental Sergeant-Major had displayed a penchant for sadistic savagery in the riding school, a savagery that I had not observed in him when we were arguing the toss with panzer and parachute divisions of the Wehrmacht. It was true that we missed the comradeship of our wartime fellow soldiers. But the compensations were many. We had a splendid barracks only half an hour's drive from Trieste, and Trieste abounded in all those things most refreshing to a soldier's palate – wine, women and song. And – prime consideration for cavalrymen – there were the horses. We had about 30 or 40, mostly captured from the Germans, Hungarians or Cossacks, and they varied from tough little Russian animals, ideal for teaching the young entry, to pure bred Hanoverian mares, which would have been the envy of any horse coper. Equestrian activity was continuous. Aiello racecourse had been developed to Sandown standards; there was show-jumping, hunter trials, hacking over the wonderful stone-wall country of Venezia Giulia, and, of course, riding school!

How we suffered! The old cries of 'Who told you to dismount?' or 'Is the horse all right?' rang out once more. To trot endlessly without stirrups, or endure a blanket ride, or go down a line of fences with folded arms and no stirrups – these things were our daily fare, and we thereby learned a lot – how to sit well down in the saddle, improve our hands, drive a horse into his fences, and, most important, the niceties of horse management, for there is nothing like grooming a horse yourself, mucking out, feeding and watering, and seeing to the tack to make you understand and appreciate what the grooms do for your beloved animals.

Having arrived at the Adjutant's office in answer to the Colonel's summons, I now waited apprehensively before being ushered into the presence, unaware that our equestrian sporting calendar was shortly to be enlarged and enhanced. Moreover, the Colonel's first words put any nagging conscience of guilt to rest. 'Ah, John. Sit down.'

'Thank you, Colonel.'

'You speak Italian, don't you!'

It was not a question, but a statement. I acknowledged some superficial acquaintance with the vernacular.

'Right, I want you to go and buy a fox.'

In the British Army, orders have long been a basis for discussion, or as Wellington put it: 'Nobody in the British army ever reads a regulation or an order . . . in any other manner than as an amusing novel.' But my commanding officer was not one of those with whom it would have been prudent to make too much of these democratic tendencies. I could think of nothing better than: 'Very good, Colonel.' He was, however, good enough to offer two further pieces of information, both useful and one reassuring.

'Loopy[1] is flying back from England with seven couple of foxhounds, and we're going to start a drag round the Basovizia country. So we must

[1] See note on page 23: at this time Major Loopy Kennard was a squadron leader.

have a smell. Understand? The PRI[2] will go up to twenty quid.'

I saluted and withdrew. Now where the devil was I to find a fox, and even if I did, how would I get it back to the kennels, which, I learned from the Adjutant, were to be established near the stables? All my powers of leadership, resolution, cunning, haggling and indeed fluency in Italian would be put to the test. I repaired first to the mess. This was a problem best discussed over a mid-morning glass of Madeira *and a map*. Thus armed, I would be able to do what all soldiers did when faced with insoluble difficulties – make an appreciation of the situation.

I had heard tell of foxes that lurked and preyed in the foothills near Gorizia and it was there that I would start my search. I set forth in a 15-cwt truck *with* a good, reliable driver – the wisdom of taking a driver with me was to be firmly established before long. My additional equipment was composed of an Italian dictionary, a haversack ration, brewing-up kit and 25,000 lire[3]. Thus furnished I launched myself in pursuit of the uneatable. The first farmer I visited was an old acquaintance with whom I had done previous business buying forage. After customary exchanges and the downing of some glasses of roughish Marsala, I got to the point:

'*Vorrei comprare una volpe.*'

'*Cosa?*'

'*Vorrei comprare una volpe.*'

'*Perchè?*'

I launched into an explanation of why I wanted to buy a fox and this meant going into some detail about the particular form of *la caccia* which we intended to pursue. Maurizio, the farmer, knew something about fox-hunting. Having been a soldier himself and stationed near Rome, he had been to the famous cavalry school at Tor di Quinto and seen the hounds at exercise. But as I stumbled over the unlikely complexities of acquiring a fox so that its urine could be collected and applied to a pad which would then be dragged by a man on foot over the stone-wall country near Basovizia – all with a view to enabling foxhounds and ourselves, suitably mounted and accoutred, to chase after this scent – Maurizio looked at me sideways. I floundered on, but he was already shaking his head. 'I don't

[2] President of Regimental Institutes, usually the Regimental Second-in-Command who held the purse-strings.

[3] In those days the lire was worth much more than now, about 1,000 to £1.

think, my friend,' was the purport of his message, 'that I can help you to catch a wild animal so that you can keep it in captivity in order to store up its *orina*'.

I accepted defeat, drank another glass of Marsala, trying not to compare it with the fluid we had just been discussing, and departed. Before leaving, I got out of him the information that Giuseppe, 15 kilometres further on towards Udine, might help, as he had an absolute passion for *la caccia* and was always going out with a gun. One look at Giuseppe's wife was enough to explain his passion for something else, but it was clear from her manner that she owned the farm. A change of tactics seemed sensible, so I made it clear, simply and bluntly, that I needed a fox and was willing to pay 15,000 lire for it. He reached for his gun and a grimy game bag, which, judging by its rattling bulges, was full of cartridges. '*Andiamo!*' No, I explained, a live one. His face fell. '*Perchè?*'

Once bitten, twice shy. I asked the direct question. 'Do you know where I can buy a live fox?'

'*Mi scusi, no.*'

'*Grazie, e a rivadella.*'

Two coverts drawn – two blank. Would the third time be lucky? We drove on to the village of Maiello, where, during the last unforgettable days of the war when my squadron of 4th Hussars was with the New Zealanders in that glorious gallop from the Senio to Padova, and on towards the Austrian border, I had stayed two nights and had my concentration seriously disrupted by a tawny-eyed *ragazza* who tried to persuade me that wherever I went, I would need a 'laundress'. In Maiello I found an old friend, Giacomo, a former Partisan leader, now respectably managing a bank. He exuded confidence. '*Una volpe? Sì, naturalmente. Andiamo!*' We climbed into the truck.

'*Dove?*' I asked.

'*Sempre diritto.*' Straight on.

We drove straight on, straight on to Udine, to Pordenone, to Conegliano, to Treviso, to Mestre. I had to fork out lots of lire for *benzina* and for glasses of Soave, but it was worth it. At Mestre we drove straight into the Piazza Centrale where the great caravans and lorries of a circus were all parked together. *Il padrone* was summoned and the three of us invaded a *trattoria*. Wine was called for and the situation once more explained. A fox, a live fox, was instantly required by *il Capitano*

Strawson. Never mind why. *Il Colonello* demanded a fox. But the circus owner was insistent. He had to know why. In a flash of irritation – or was it inspiration? – I snapped a quick reply. 'The Colonel always eats roast fox for supper.'

'*Magnifico!*' My hand was seized and pumped. Only the *Cavalleria Inglesi* could produce such men – the lions of Europe who hunted and ate foxes, while milder-minded Italians had to content themselves with shooting larks and sparrows. '*Bravissimo! Ancora una bottiglia!*' I was beginning to be worried about my store of lire. Would there be enough left?

Triumphantly we returned to the piazza. Orders were bellowed, underlings began running about, and ten minutes later a huge cage was produced and inside it was a big, reddish dog fox, snarling, leaping, frantically seeking a way out of his dreadful prison. At this, my heart sank. Could I really be a party to such violation of nature? But orders were orders and duty was duty. I handed over the lire, the *padrone* bellowed at a vast mountain of a woman – his wife or the circus's fat lady? – to bring *una bottiglia*. I could not refuse, but thanked my foresight in bringing a driver. Then back we went, returning Giacomo to Maiello and so on to our Opicina barracks, which we reached at midnight. The guard commander did not take kindly to my demand for overnight accommodation for the fox in the guard-room, so I sent for the Orderly Officer, who arrived twenty minutes later with every sign of being hurriedly dressed and in a poor humour.

'Giles,' I asked him, 'have you had dinner?'

'Of course!'

'Well, in the back of this truck you will find a fox who has not yet dined. He wishes to. What's more he requires bedding and some sort of modification made to his stabling so that whenever he pees, every drop of the precious fluid will be channelled down some kind of funnel into an eagerly waiting urn below. Well, see to it!' I was glad to reflect that in this era of the return to real soldiering, there was no danger of my orders not being carried out to the letter. The best thing of all about it was that the fox's captivity did not last long. By judicious dieting the fox, known as Fred after his lookalike member of the sergeants' mess, Fred Fox MM, supplied us with such a store of smell that the Colonel endorsed my proposal that he should be released. I was thus able to comfort myself with

the thought that by finding the fox at Mestre in the first place, I was enabled to give him back his freedom. We took him out one night to Basovizia and set him free. With one last look back at us, he made off across a field towards the Yugoslav border.

In retrospect, I could not help reflecting that far from it being thought of as uneatable, it was my chance declaration that a fox was an irresistibly dainty dish to set before a colonel that seemed to have clinched the deal and crowned my pursuit with success. And we have the evidence of Peter Mayle to support this view. In his *A Year in Provence*, his rascally neighbour, Massot, tells Mayle that after skinning the fox, removing its *parties*, eliminating the *goût savage* by running cold water over it for a day, you hang it, put it in a casserole, immerse it in a mixture of red wine and blood, add herbs, onion and garlic, then after simmering for two days and with the aid of *pommes frites – voilà*.

It was by now clear to me that if you're going to have much to do with draghounds, you need to be a versatile sort of fellow. Just how versatile I had still to learn. I had succeeded in running a fox to earth and by doing so had been able to give that very same fox its freedom. My next assignment was to act as courier to some of the very draghounds whose duty it would be to pursue his undeniably strong scent. When our first season's draghunting was over at the end of March 1946, I was allowed two weeks' leave in England, and towards the end of it, there arrived a dramatic telegram from the Colonel. It seemed that our pack of draghounds was to be reinforced in readiness for future sport, and some bitches were required for breeding. 'An extra week's leave granted', read the telegram, 'if you bring back Thankful, Vital and Sapphire from . . .' the name of a well-known pack of Buckinghamshire hounds followed. When the Colonel offered to do something for you provided some condition was fulfilled, you knew that his apparent openhandedness concealed a requirement that you did as you were told. I therefore had little choice in the matter. There was nothing to do but accept the challenge and enjoy my extra days of freedom. It was as well that I had no idea what was coming.

My first step was to arrange with the movement staff of the War Office to change the date of my travel documents which would authorise first class passage from Victoria Station via Dover and Calais to Villach in Austria where a regimental truck would meet me for the final leg to Trieste. Next I spoke by telephone to the Hunt kennels to announce when I would collect the hounds. The kennel-huntsman advised me to bring some couples with me, that is, sets of leather collars joined by a chain so that hounds could be 'coupled'. Then they could move along together and would be easier to control. My mother had been warned that one and a half couple of foxhounds would be spending one night at her London flat so that I could get to Victoria Station early on the following morning. Thus on the afternoon before my journey I set off to the kennels in a hired car complete with driver.

The kennel-huntsman was clearly sad to be parting with his beloved hounds. 'Where be they going?' he asked.

'To Trieste.'

'Eh?'

'To northern Italy.'

'Ah! Be there foxes there?'

I toyed for a moment with the idea of telling him about my previous adventure, but thought better of it. 'Yes,' I said, 'but what we've got there is a drag.' He shook his head, Cassandra-like, and gave the three bitches a farewell pat, to which some vigorous stern waving was the response. What he did not tell me was that he had fed the hounds some hours before. We climbed into the car, myself in front with the driver, the three foxhounds on the back seat. Before we had driven far along bumpy, twisting roads, the most appalling thing happened. Thankful, Vital and Sapphire deposited the nourishment recently received at the kennels all over the back seat and were now huddled in the space immediately behind us. I thought at once that this would mean a devastating addition to the fare and began to express profuse apologies to the driver. To my relief and astonishment, he was smiling. 'This isn't my car,' he chortled. 'It's the governor's.'

It was fortunate that my mother's ground floor flat had a small garden to which the hounds could from time to time repair. But there was also the matter of feeding them. At that time there was, of course, a shortage of meat in England. When my charges had demolished the fortnight's ration and all the bread, they reported to me, and for the first time in my life I was able to sympathise with the outraged dignity of Mr Bumble when Oliver Twist had the unmitigated insolence to ask for more. Next morning we set off. Nothing untoward had occurred as the four of us disembarked from the London taxi at Victoria, my three bitches properly accoutred with couples and leads. But at the station I encountered my first stumbling block. The railway transport officer categorically refused to permit us on the military train. My appeals to his sporting instinct – and he was after all a major of His Majesty's Foot Guards – were in vain. There was nothing for it but to telephone the Horse Guards, that is Headquarters London District, under whose authority this officer carried out his duties. Happily I spoke to a colonel of Household Cavalry responsible for administrative affairs, who, in turn, had a 'few words' with the RTO. His opposition was instantly transformed into active co-operation, and before long I found myself in possession of a reserved compartment with the foxhounds comfortably occupying the whole of one seat while I reclined opposite them.

So far, so good. Yet at Dover, in the person of an embarkation officer, I encountered a will so inflexible that I began to understand what Philip

Faulconbridge had meant when he declared that even if the three corners of the world came in arms, yet we would shock them. No argument, no threat could prevail. He was adamant that we were not to be allowed on the military steamer. I could not but recall that 'man, proud man, Dressed in a little brief authority . . . Plays such fantastic tricks before high heaven, As make the angels weep'. But this was no time for weeping. To be thus thwarted almost before I had really got going was unthinkable. Sterner measures were called for. There was nothing for it but to purchase one human and three canine tickets for the next Golden Arrow boat shortly sailing for Calais. I then informed the embarkation officer of our intention to catch the next tide. As we passed the gangway of the military steamer, he was there, guarding it with a posse of Redcaps. Giving him a gravely ironic salute, I led the way to the far more comfortable quarters to which our Golden Arrow tickets entitled us. On board I was greeted as something of a hero. It was not every day that foxhounds sailed for the Adriatic coast. A retired cavalryman, who looked as if he might have hunted in the Peninsula with Wellington's pack, pronounced it to be a jolly sporting show. A pretty woman, who had observed the iron hand with which I maintained discipline over my three charges – they as a result playing the sycophant in a way most pleasing to my self-esteem – and who, perhaps, wistfully indulged in daydreams of being similarly ruled, invited me to bring my hounds to Paris. I regretfully declined, feeling I had enough on my hands.

At Calais the Customs and Immigration officials were at first incredulous. There was a good deal of hand gesticulation, shoulder shrugging and consultation of the next senior man. I understood only too well what Major Thompson had meant by the sweet land of mistrust. My attempt to explain the situation in French simply added to the confusion. At length an English-speaking official was blown for and we got down to brass tacks.

'What are you doing with these dogs?'

'I'm taking them to join my regiment.'

'What for?'

'For breeding purposes.'

'Breeding?'

'Yes. To reinforce the pack, to get some little ones, some puppies.'

'But why do you want puppies?'

'So that they can grow up, become big and strong and entirely suitable for, well, *la chasse*.'

'But what are you going to hunt?'

'We aren't. The hounds will follow a smell.'

'The smell?'

'Yes. What we do is this.' I then described the whole process of laying on a day with the drag – the meet, the stirrup-cup, the runner, moving off, releasing hounds at the start of the first leg, and so on, right through to throwing hounds the worry and sounding the kill. 'The stone-wall country of Basovizia', I concluded, 'is absolutely ideal for the drag.'

'Basovizia?'

'Yes, it's near Trieste.'

'You mean you are taking these dogs to Italy?'

'Yes, of course. The regiment is stationed there.'

A great light came over the official's countenance. He briefed his colleagues. From then on nothing could have been too much trouble for them. An underling was even dispatched to the local knacker to procure much needed flesh for my now ravenous companions. It was just as well for my Calais problems were not yet over. I now had to get on the military train for Villach. Again stalemate. The railway staff would not hear of it, and, after a day and a night in the local transit camp, it was clear to me that a kennel-huntsman earns his wages. Thankful, Vital and Sapphire seemed content with this temporary stopover. Regular victuals from the camp-cookhouse, adequate exercise – more than adequate for me as I had to keep them coupled, and I did not like to think of the Colonel's reaction if they had gone spare in Calais – and comfortable quarters. They had never had it so good! But time was slipping by. Then fortune smiled on me for the Director of Movement from the War Office, a keen hunting man, arrived on a tour of inspection. Delighted with the whole plan, he gave orders that as an empty train was returning to Villach that afternoon, the four of us could go too. Things were looking up. At Victoria we had had a compartment to ourselves. Now we had a complete train. I settled down comfortably. The worst was over; at Villach there would be the regimental truck which met most trains; the thing was as good as done. My confidence was premature for the climacteric moments of the journey were still to come.

Late that evening the train halted at some minor station in eastern

France to take on water or fuel. It was not an official halt and might be for only a short time. But I decided to take advantage of the train's equilibrium, and to have 'a wash and brush up'. Taking off my tunic, with soap and towel in my hand, I cautioned my charges to be on their best behaviour and advanced along the corridor. Almost at once I was distracted by a commotion behind me. An inquisitive member of the station staff had entered the train and opened the door of my compartment and before he could shut it again, one of the hounds, Thankful, was in the corridor. In front of my horrified eyes she leaped out on to the platform and set off down it at a rate which would have warmed the heart of her old kennel-huntsman in Buckinghamshire. As she ran, she gave tongue, but to my ears it was not the musical discord, the sweet thunder that Hippolyta recalled to Theseus – it was the voice of doom.

There are, as we know, moments when contemplation is out of place and circumstances cry out for action. This was one of them. Yelling a terrible curse at the culprit, I sprang wildly to the platform and launched myself in pursuit. As I ran I could not help reflecting that here was a drag hunt in reverse, not hound chasing runner, but runner desperately trying to overhaul hound. Right down the length of the platform we went and as we approached the barrier, I shouted exhortations to ticket collectors to stop the runaway. No good! They withdrew from our path with the same precision, the same dexterity which the matador employs to evade the charging bull. We scattered the few natives who were in the main part of the station, and my quarry, who perhaps for the first time knew what it was like to be hunted, made for the exit. As I dashed down the steps into the road, I heard the guard's whistle blow, at once echoed by the train's shrill emission of steam. I was trapped, not by two pursuers, but by two escapers.

Yes, that was the position. On the one hand there was, Thankful, eagerly hunting some imaginary scent. To abandon her in a country barbarous enough not to understand the business of hunting would be to write finis to my career as a cavalryman. On the other hand, the train was on the point of departure with my other two charges, my luggage and my identity card – in France the only acceptable proof that a man is alive. In the middle was myself, coatless and thus moneyless, breathless from running, surrounded by hostile and suspicious strangers, not particularly proficient in the vernacular, with the single consolatory thought that as my soap and towel were in my hand, I would at least be able to wash myself without incurring expenditure of any sort.

A hopeless situation, you might think. Perhaps so, but if there were no reinforcement to be gained from hope, think what resolution I could gain from despair. Outside the station my hound faltered. A moment later she realised that those who hesitate are saved. My hand closed like a vice on her stern, I heaved her into my arms and retraced my steps – at the double. As I threw myself into the all but moving train, a train conducting officer appeared in the corridor. He patted the bitch. 'She's a nice girl,' he said, 'What's her name?'

'She's Thankful,' I croaked, 'and, by heaven, so am I.'

After this stormy scene the rest of the journey was something of an anticlimax. But when I handed over my three companions to the kennels, I was able to make my way to my quarters with the satisfaction of having earned my extra week's leave. Subsequent breeding successes were all that they should have been, and many were the happy days of drag-hunting that we had with our horses and hounds at Basovizia. There was no doubt that these beloved animals provided us with what Whyte Melville called the best of our fun.

But now we are told by Roger Scruton[4] that the majority of those who go out hunting are women – 'And this is the real reason why hunting is so full of terrors, and why you need nerves of steel to cope with it.' He goes on to describe what he calls the 'hunting harpy', a kind of self-appointed vigilante, who is always in the right, and who will bellow at you no matter whether you are in front of her at a fence or behind her. It will be either 'Get out of the way' or 'Do please mind my heels'. On the other hand Scruton concedes that not all hunting women are harpies, and that many of those taking part combine in their appearance and performance the fearlessness, elegance, grace and skill which we so much admire and which enhance the hunting field. This is how I like to think of them and we might now turn our attention to their schooling and management.

---

[4] *On Hunting* by Roger Scruton (Yellow Jersey Press, 1998).

7

Love in the Drag-hunting Field

'When a man's trying a young filly, his hands can't be too light.
A touch too much will bring her on her haunches, or throw
her out of her step. She should hardly feel the iron in her
mouth. But when I've got to do with a trained mare, I always
choose that she shall know I'm there. Their mouths are never
so fine then, and they generally want to be brought up to the
bit . . . and when she comes to her fences, give her her head;
but steady at first, and make her know you're there . . . And
look here, Clavvy; ride her with spurs. Let her know they're
on; and if she tries to get her head, give 'em her. Yes, by George,
giv 'em her.'

Captain Boodle to Captain Clavering in Trollope's
The Claverings

'*Love in the
Mist*'

120

Those unfamiliar with the context of this passage will readily understand that in offering this advice to his friend, Captain Boodle is recommending a technique, wrapped up in equine metaphor, designed to forward the pursuit and conquest of a *two-legged* mare. It was advice which might profitably have been followed by one of my drag-hunting companions, whom I will call Jasper Curb. Curb was a heavy dragoon, a breed never renowned for intellectual nimbleness, but a fine horseman, who loved and almost lived for horses. He was a goodly specimen, tall, lithe, with a sense of humour considerably less ponderous than his moustache, and was at his best mounted. Nature had not overplayed her hand, however, for not only did he border on being inarticulate, but his actual process of reasoning left much to be desired. At the time when he used to ride the Staff College drag-lines in my company he was a bachelor, but nevertheless firmly supported the traditional view of matrimony which held good for cavalry regiments: A captain *may* marry; a major *should*; a colonel *must!* Curb confided in me that as he had achieved his majority, he had decided to have a go at following this matrimonial dictum. But at his first attempt, made at a recent hunt ball, he had encountered a disappointing check. His partner that evening had been a long-standing female friend, a good hunting girl and by no means a harpy, and it seemed the coalition of romantic music, champagne cup and the alluring, proximity of his lady love had brought Curb to a pitch of fervour and boldness which would brook no denial. The lady was not exactly young, well into her thirties and, although prematurely grey-haired, still comely. Moreover, as Lord Chiltern's hunting friend Mr Spooner would have put it: 'She's such a well-built creature! There's a look of blood about her I don't see in any of 'em. That sort of breeding is what one wants to get through the mud with.' In any event Curb had taken the plunge and proposed marriage. The lady in question, incapable, as some of them are, of answering questions of this sort with a simple, uncompromising affirmative – or negative – shied and simpered before asking why he wanted to marry her. Naturally self-effacing, eschewing a tender and reassuring word of love, clearly not briefed by Captain Boodle, he mumbled something about her recalling the memory of a dear old grey mare he had once had. He was capable of no greater compliment. She, however, did not see it in this light, and when after further sharp exchanges it was revealed that the mare in question was not even a dapple grey, it will readily be understood that his suit did not prosper at all thereafter.

I took his disappointment to heart and soon afterwards was able to propose a remedy. We were both walking round a hunter trial course before competing, and we came to a particularly unpleasant-looking fence. I commented that it was unreasonably stiff, but Curb simply gazed at it with enviable sang-froid and announced that one wouldn't think twice about it out hunting. He had told me that he was still determined to find some suitable stable-companion, as apart from this duty being expected of a major, he had high hopes in the future of commanding his regiment, and 'A colonel must, you know'. Yet he had no particular creature in mind. He was on the look-out for *any* suitable partner. As we stood by the fence an extremely pretty girl thundered towards it on a big bay horse, and miraculously retained her seat when it refused. She took the animal back some 20 yards, administered the appropriate correction, and then, approaching the fence again with proper persuasion, cleared it beautifully. Bearing in mind Curb's so far fruitless quest for companionship, and noting from the hunter trial programme that the girl was still a filly, I turned to him and pointed out that there was the very one to make him the happiest of men. He shook his head mournfully. 'If a woman handles horses like that', he objected, 'think how she'd handle me.'

How Curb would have envied Surtees's Mr Waffles, of whom it was said that:

> No fox had been hunted by more hounds than Waffles had been by the ladies; but though he had chatted and prattled with fifty fair maids – any one of whom he might have found difficult to resist, if *pinned* single-handed by, in a country house, yet the multiplicity of assailants completely neutralised each other, and verified the truth of the adage that there is *safety in a crowd*.'

In this manner Waffles had been able to resist pretty, lisping Miss Wordsworth in spite of the arrow she shot into his heart, for this had been removed by the dart from Mary Ogleby's dark eyes, only in its turn to be neutralised when the commanding presence and noble looks of the Honourable Miss Letitia Amelia Susannah Jemimah de Jenkins made themselves felt, only to forfeit their influence when some even more bewitching creature appeared on the scene. Now Waffles had become Master of the Laverick Wells Hounds, and as he had money to spend, not only did he see to it that his huntsman, Tom Towler, was mounted on hundred-guinea horses, but his general magnificence ensured that 'many elegant and interesting young ladies . . . took to riding in fan-tailed habits and feathered hats, and talking about leaping and hunting, and riding over rails'. And it was to Laverick Wells and Mr Waffles's hounds that our friend, Soapey Sponge, brought his two immortal animals, Hercules and Multum in Parvo, under the practised hand of his groom, Peter Leather, where they all created such a sensation that, as Leather told his master, 'the men are all mad and the women all wild to see you'. But, as Surtees shrewdly reminds us, nothing puts people's backs up so readily as the idea that a stranger is coming amongst them to take the shine out of them across country, and by dint of getting old Tom Towler thoroughly tipsy with glasses of port and brandy-and-water, Mr Waffles and his hunting friends persuade the huntsman to have a drag over the stiffest parts of the country in order that Mr Sponge and his mount could be tested to the full. Moreover, they would make a point of ensuring that Mr Sponge was led into mischief.

Surtees's comments on and description of drag-hunting are too good to be missed. In the first place it presents what he calls 'conveniences for neck-breaking' in the sort of circumstances presented by Mr Ackermann's shop windows, in other words by ensuring that all the big places in fences are to be tackled. The scent itself can be of any strength, so that there is no hesitation on the part of hounds. They will run as if they were tied to the scent, which can itself be trailed in order to include all the most dangerous places in the country, enabling those negotiating them to declare that they never saw such fences in their lives. In short, as Peter Beckford put it, if the object is hard riding, a trail scent is just the thing.

It was just as well that the discerning Peter Leather knew what he was about for he was able to warn Mr Sponge as he mounted Hercules that: 'they're a goin' to run a drag to try what he's made on, so be on the look-out'. As Sponge rides through the town to make his way to the meet, he comes in for a good deal of censure from those observing him. The ladies confide in one another that he is a 'fright', while secretly admiring him. The men who are going to hunt with him are dismayed at the masterly way in which Sponge bestrides his noble beast, but still long for the conceit to be taken out of him before night. At the meet itself, Tom Towler, the huntsman, is regarded by children as the greatest man in the world;

keepers, millers, pedestrian sportsmen exchange confidences; grooms rectify any derangements which their masters' horses or furniture may have suffered before handing them over to their scarlet-clad riders; a black bottle and glass are passed round; the ladies, whether on horseback or in flys, prattle and inquire after Mr Sponge; and, greatest of ironies, 'the hounds, which they had all come to see, were never looked at'.

But now Mr Waffles jerks his head at Tom Towler, and Tom, getting his hounds together, with the whips round them, bustles away for the covert, with the field in their various ways – some fearful, some joyful, all anxious – responding to the *twang, twang, twang* of Tom Towler's horn as, from the wood, he sees his hounds streaming away after the laid scent he knew he would find there. Then the race – for this is what it amounts to – begins for the fifteen or twenty horsemen willing to risk their animals and their necks. The pace is awful, but Mr Sponge, with Hercules striding well and leaping safely, is well up behind Tom Towler, crashing through stiffish fences, hounds going faster and faster, fence after fence negotiated, including a big stone wall and a formidable brook, while prudently giving a desperate black bullfinch, too thick to see through, a miss when a nearby gate is conveniently opened for them. At the end of the run there are but five or six horsemen left, one of whom had plunged heavily into the brook and now resembled a water rat, but all of them recognised now that Mr Sponge was not only a courageous rider, but a skilled one too. So while Tom Towler goes off with his hounds, re-emerging from the other side of a hill nearby to complete the farce of it having been a genuine hunt, Mr Waffles greets Sponge as the hero of the run, and they all exult in congratulating themselves in having completed 7 miles in 21 minutes – an estimate which, in the manner of Falstaff exaggerating the number of his assailants in buckram suits, soon became 9 miles in 25 minutes, and at length, having done the rounds of the country, finished up as a run of 33 miles in one hour and 40 minutes!

Although Mr Sponge may have won a great victory while drag-hunting with the Laverick Wells Hounds, when it came to a later hunt, this time mounted on Multum in Parvo and out with Sir Harry Scattercash's Nonsuch Hounds, it was to be Soapey himself who would be vanquished. Like all the other sportsmen present, Mr Sponge had admired the way in which Miss Lucy Glitters handled her Arab palfrey with light hands, a gentle touch of the whip and thorough control. Indeed she looked beautiful on horseback. Although Sponge is somewhat put out by Multum in Parvo's refusal to jump a hand-gate leading from the shrubberies into the park – preferring to 'walk through the gate, as if it had been made of paper' – he none the less has earned Miss Glitters's gratitude by clearing the way for her. But when it comes to clearing the park-palings, Multum in Parvo sets a fine example, gets over with a rap, giving Lucy just the lead she needs to follow. On they go together over frozen fallows, over more fences and through a rasper 'without disturbing a twig'. It is definitely a good thing and Sponge 'went crashing on, now over high places, now over low, just as they came in his way, closely followed by the fair Lucy Glitters. The huntsman, Mr Watchorn, who is tiring of the sport, is lost in admiration as he observes Sponge taking a stiff flight of rails, even though a gap is nearby, again closely followed by Lucy, and declares 'I never see'd sich a man as that! Nor woman nouther!' And when they find themselves confronted by a broad mill-course with a very stiff fence on the taking-off side, Sponge brushes through it and somehow gets over the water, exhorting Lucy to 'Run him at it!', and when she successfully does so declaring 'Well done! you're a trump.' It is auguring well for romance, and as by this time the two of them are practically in charge of hounds, despite Mr Watchorn's anger and frustration at losing control, at the end of the run, as Sponge comes up to Lucy and is:

> . . . looking at her bewitching eyes, her lovely face, and feeling the sweet fragrance of her breath, a something shot through Mr Sponge's pull-devil, pull-baker coat, his corduroy waistcoat, his Eureka shirt, Angola[1] vest, and penetrated the very cockles of his heart. He gave her such a series of smacking kisses as startled her horse and astonished a poacher who happened to be hid in the adjoining hedge.

It was clear that he had got it badly. He had never felt so happy.

As he eyed his angelic charmer, her lustrous eyes, her glowing cheeks, her pearly teeth, the bewitching fulness of her elegant *tournure*, and thought of the masterly way she rode the run – above all, of the dashing style in which she

---

[1] Today we would say Angora – Angola being a corruption of Angora, a town in Asia Minor – to describe fabric made from the wool of the angora goat.

charged the mill-race – he felt something quite different to anything he had experienced with any of the buxom widows or lackadaisical misses, whom he could just love or not . . . Miss Glitters, he knew, had nothing, and yet he felt he could not do without her.

Unlike the fate of my old friend, Jasper Curb, Soapey Sponge's intoxication *did* lead to matrimonial bliss. What better instance is there of love in the hunting field! What is more, the bolt of Cupid does not confine its target to mere mortals mounted on horseback. For what does Somerville say:

> Mark well the wanton females of thy pack,
> That curl their taper tails, and frisking court
> Their pyebald mates enamour'd: their red eyes

Flash fires impure; nor rest nor food they take,
Goaded by furious love. In separate cells
Confine them now, lest bloody civil wars
Annoy thy peaceful state.

Peter Beckford is very conscious of this warning in offering his own advice as to breeding hounds, and tells us to watch over the bitches with caution and separate those that are going to be difficult, for it is not only love they wish to make, but mischief too, which can set the whole kennel by the ears and cause even death among your best hounds. Beckford, like Somerville, believed that it was only in the UK that the perfect hound, both in scent and speed, could be bred, and it was therefore necessary to 'consider the size, shape, colour, constitution, and natural disposition, of the dog you breed from, as well as the fineness of his nose, his stoutness, and method of hunting'. He is specific in his advice. He advocates the judicious cross, even recommending that the cross most beneficial to a foxhound is the beagle – 'a handsome, bony, tender-nosed, stout beagle would, occasionally, be no improper cross for a high-bred pack of foxhounds'. Do not put an old dog to an old bitch. Breed only from healthy hounds and so ensure healthy offspring. The early months of the year are best for breeding – January, February and March – and when the bitches increase, let them not hunt for the safety of both bitch and puppies.

Beckford also tells us that sometimes the excuse is offered that hounds will not hunt a cold scent because they were *too high bred*, but he thinks it more likely that they are *too ill-bred*. In any event it is the sound judgement of the breeder and the subsequent patience and skill of the huntsman that produce the best hounds. In the case of draghounds, of course, most packs are made up of foxhounds drafted from other packs around the country. It is relatively rare to find such emphasis placed on hound breeding as with the Berks and Bucks, while, as I have described, we reinforced our 4th Hussars pack of draghounds with Thankful, Vital and Sapphire because of the need to breed and keep our pack to the level of seven or eight couple. And in any event the scent of a drag-line is powerful enough for any hound to hunt it.

It will be remembered that Mr Harkaway regarded his hounds with something like worship. It was they who did all the work, while the men and horses, however necessary they might be to the sport, could but observe and conform to what the hounds were up to. Praise for his hounds delighted Mr Harkaway, whereas compliments about his horses meant little. Most of us, however, will probably endorse Mr Jorrocks's declaration about loving both, although, as I have indicated already, for me the horse had always been the greatest joy of following hounds. I have related how my beautiful mare Bella carried me so boldly and well during my service as MDH. Now I would like to pay tribute to another four-legged friend.

'I could say such wonderful things to you'

128

8
Four-legged Friends

Where in this wide world can man find nobility without pride,
friendship without envy, or beauty without vanity? Here,
where grace is laced with muscle, and strength by gentleness
confined. He serves without servility, he has fought without
enmity. There is nothing so powerful, nothing less violent;
there is nothing so quick, nothing more patient. England's past
has been borne on his back. All our history is his industry. We
are his heirs, he our inheritance.

Ronald Duncan

All those familiar with this splendid tribute to the horse will no doubt
be conscious of how very apt it is when applied to one or more of
their own four-legged friends. One of the great bonuses which many of us
have enjoyed because of drag-hunting is that our beloved animal has also
given us much joy when indulging in associated equestrian activities –
hunter trials, show-jumping or point-to-pointing. This brings me to the
story of Hungry. Hungry, you will recall, was the horse I was going to visit

in his loose box when the Colonel blew for me and charged me to go in pursuit of the uneatable. He was a beautiful animal, a bay gelding about five years old, and we found him in Austria while setting up, of all things, a prisoner of war camp *for horses*. It came about like this. When the German armies in Italy surrendered at the beginning of May 1945, the regiment was ordered to Austria, and one of the duties given to my squadron was to set up a camp near Lienz at which we would receive and take charge of Cossack and Hungarian cavalry brigades which had fought on the German side. In command of this camp was a brother officer, Claud, who might have been made for the job. Lean, fit, a man of few words but infinite determination, he had been Joint Master of the famous Black and Tan pack of foxhounds in County Limerick before the war. He was the only horseman I ever knew who would frequently, from choice, ride bareback, and had even on one occasion, when his favourite hunter had a girth gall, hunted hounds without a saddle. Not many men could have done that over the formidable banks of the Scarteen country.

When the war came he at once enlisted in the Household Cavalry as a trooper. At this time there was still a mounted part of the regiment and he was sensible enough on joining simply to admit to a previous acquaintance with horses. Too many recruits had regretted their claim to 'know how to ride' when the moment came that they were invited to see whether they could ride 'this one'. Then an animal mild in appearance, but an expert in getting rid of anyone on its back, would be led from the stables to provide a few moments of *Schadenfreude* for the onlookers. But Claud was not allowed to stay as a trooper for long. His natural appetite for command and his uncanny tactical sense soon demanded that he should lead, not follow. And so he joined the 4th Hussars as a troop leader and happily was in the same squadron as myself. It was under his guidance that I was able to improve my equestrian ability. He was a man who understood and loved animals, and had a way with them that I had never seen in anyone else. He would croon and talk to horses and they would do anything he asked them. It might be said that he was a forerunner to Monty Roberts, the Horse Whisperer. So it was wholly fitting that to Claud fell the job of running our POW camp for horses.

It was my task to visit him from time to time to see what was needed in the way of forage, veterinary stores, straw for bedding, shoes for the horses and clothing for his Cossacks and Hungarians. Sometimes I would accompany him as he rode round on his tour of inspection together with his staff of senior, formerly enemy, officers. His method of command seemed to require little talking, for he spoke no Russian, Hungarian or German, nor were his subordinates fluent in English. This state of affairs ensured that only absolute essentials justified verbal exchanges, delivered it seemed in a series of horse-like grunts, complemented if necessary with signs or paper drawings. Great contentment reigned throughout the camp. It was clear enough why. Enemies some weeks before, the British Commandant and his assistants had one great thing in common – love of horses. The whole camp was run for their benefit. Each squadron had its own horse lines, its own huge grazing area, its own exercise routine, its own watering places at the nearby river, and its own parades for inspection. Karinthia at that time of year, the end of May, is always beautiful. It was made doubly so by the task in hand.

When I accompanied him on his tour of inspection, he would insist that, like himself, I rode without a saddle, something not really to my taste although it greatly improved my seat. We would ride from squadron to squadron, straight across country with usually a few ditches to negotiate en route. The squadron leader would come forward, already mounted, salute, explain the state of his horses and men, produce any animals for special notice and discuss the next few days' programme. It was on one such visit that, much to our surprise, one of the Hungarian officers reported to us in a state of great agitation. It seemed that on their way to our camp – for they had all made their own way to us on orders from higher command – the Hungarian colonel's favourite charger had broken loose during a halt not far distant from the camp, galloped away and, in spite of searchings, had not been recovered. He was by all accounts a beauty, big, bold, tough, good over fences and fast. *Now* there had come a rumour from one of the villages nearby that a horse of this description had been seen in a field some miles away. Several farmers, it was said, had approached him. None had succeeded in catching him. Without more ado, three of us set off – Claud, a Hungarian soldier who could identify the horse, and myself. We went in a 3-ton truck with another horse in it, a head collar and bridle, grooming kit, some water and a few pounds of oats. Full of hope, we arrived at the village where the horse had been reported to have been seen. Yes, we were told, he was still there, in a large field by the river, but he was wild, we were warned. No one could get near him. He would kick and bite, not even waiting for a would-be capturer to approach, but launch an attack as soon as *his* field was entered.

We explained our mission. There were some sceptics among the villagers. The farmer whose field it was would certainly be glad to have the uninvited and persistent tenant evicted, and so regain possession, but what made us think we could do what all the most experienced horsemen of the district had failed to do? We made no promises, but asked to be directed to the field. Soon we were rewarded with a sight I can still recall. As we drove up and dismounted, we saw him at once. He was standing in the corner of a 20-acre field. Facing away from us, he turned his head and treated us to a look. Some 16 h.h., proud, erect, tail swishing angrily, magnificent in spite of being mud-stained, he positively glared at us. Our Hungarian soldier gave a cry of pleasure. Claud drew in his breath in open admiration. Catching him was not easy, and at first engaged the three of us. Our Hungarian friend held a bowl of corn, I stood by with the bridle, while Claud, head collar in hand, approached, making his special sort of crooning sound. This seemed to calm the animal, who whinnied and tossed his head. We moved closer, but he clearly did not like so many of us near him and reared up and dashed off, to fall cropping in a fresh spot. We changed tactics. Claud, head collar over his arm, moved forward again, with a handful of oats, again won the horse's confidence with his horse whispering act, tempted him to take the oats and slipped the head collar on. So far, so good. Next, a rope attached the head collar to a gate post, and our Hungarian soldier, who also seemed to possess some of the horse whisperer's qualities, made much of him and soothingly began some grooming. He took no objection to this and before long meekly accepted the bridle. Claud slipped quietly on to his back and rode gently round the field. Next we had to get him into the improvised horse-box. If he jibbed, we would unload the other horse and ride the two of them back to camp. But he went in like a lamb, and soon after was in Claud's own stables at camp HQ.

Once back in the ranks, so to speak, we decided to change his former unpronounceable Hungarian name. Bearing in mind, however, his native country and his seemingly insatiable appetite for oats, hay, carrots and apples, we named him *Hungry*. After a few weeks' schooling, Claud, who was shortly to return to Ireland, suggested that Hungry was the very horse for me. An impassioned plea by the Hungarian colonel, who had no wish to part with his favourite, even offering his wife as a substitute in preference to losing him, went unheeded. Hungry and I became partners, and when the regiment was ordered back to Italy in September 1945, he went with me. Thus we found ourselves together at Villa Opicina. Soon afterwards, as related earlier, Loopy Kennard brought out the foxhounds and the drag got going. But by this time several other pre-war members of the regiment had returned, having been guests of the Third Reich after the ill-fated campaign in Greece, and as both expert horsemen and connoisseurs of horseflesh, they took one look at Hungry and made it clear that my own horsemanship was not of the calibre that Hungry deserved. So Hungry usually carried either the Colonel or Loopy, the Master, over the stone-wall country of Basovizia where most of our drag-hunting was done, and he performed so well that it was agreed that he would be entered for some of the steeplechases which were beginning to be run at Aiello. Meanwhile I had to make do, it will be remembered, with Partisan, who 'pulled like the mischief'. But I was allowed to ride Hungry again, for the Colonel relented and asked me to join himself and Loopy in another regiment's hunter trial event at which three horses and riders went round together. Sandwiched between two such bold and competent horsemen, Hungry and I had the time of our lives.

So impressed was the Colonel by our performance that although I would not be permitted to ride Hungry in steeplechases, as a consolation prize I could partner him in a 6-furlong scurry at the forthcoming meeting. Ours was the first race of the afternoon and there were fourteen starters, including another regimental horse called Max, who was to be ridden by Sergeant Smith, a pre-war cavalry soldier. There were no bookmakers at the racecourse, but there was a tote – profits helped to maintain the facilities there, but it still paid out good prices. Max was the hot favourite and all the regiment's money was on him. As I mounted Hungry in the collecting ring, proudly wearing the regiment's colours of primrose and blue, I noticed how beautifully his groom had turned him out. A friend from the Queen's Bays wished me luck and asked if Hungry were worth a bet. I shook my head, not in doubt about Hungry's ability, but my own as a jockey. We cantered down to the start, came under starter's orders – butterflies very much in the stomach by this time for it was my first race ride – and we were off. To my astonishment and delight, Hungry shot straight to the front and stayed there for all 6 furlongs. Flushed with pride, making much of Hungry, I rode him back to the unsaddling enclosure, there to be greeted with sour looks from my brother officers and a bitter reproach from the friend from the Queen's Bays. The groom, on the other hand, looked overjoyed. He had reason to. Not only had his beautiful charge been victorious, but it transpired that only one ticket had been purchased at the tote in favour of Hungry. Yes, it was his and the pay-out was tremendous.

When the drag-hunting season came to a close in the spring, the Colonel made two momentous announcements. He was to leave us, retire from the service altogether and repair to his place in Dorset. And the regiment itself was to leave Italy, move to Schleswig Holstein and there await the arrival of a new commanding officer. But before either of these things happened, something that our retiring Colonel had long set his heart on would take place – a regimental point-to-point at Aiello racecourse. The Colonel

The First
Fence

134

decreed that only those who had qualified by regularly going out with the draghounds were eligible to enter, and moreover that the pre-war regimental officers were excluded – whether from motives of giving us relatively inexperienced horsemen a better chance or from sheer apprehension about racing in such dangerous company was never made clear. He did, however, permit two former rough-riding sergeant-majors of the mounted days to take part, presumably to show us the way round. There were, as I recall, eighteen starters. None of the horses, and only the two warrant officers, had ever been round a steeplechase course before. I was mounted on a reliable, but not particularly speedy, animal named Summer Star. The approach to the first fence was, to say the least of it, unnerving. If the great Duke of Wellington had been there to witness it, he would have seen nothing to reverse his criticism of the cavalry in the Peninsular campaign. He would, rather, have been confirmed in his view that the British cavalry relied too much on mere speed of movement, that there was no control of the advance, that no reserve seemed to be kept in hand. And yet we all got over it.

The really astonishing thing was that all of us, except the two rough-riding sergeant-majors, completed the course, even though towards the finish the field was spread out between half a dozen fences, and the winner was just about being led into the unsaddling enclosure by the time the last horse finished. The poor sergeant-majors, who had of course been allotted the most reluctant mounts, were then subjected to some good-natured chaff from some of the younger officers who had suffered under them in the riding school. I did not join in. I was far too conscious of the fact that they knew more about riding and schooling horses, and horse management generally, than would ever be my lot. But our regimental point-to-point was a fitting finale to our equitational adventures in Venezia Giulia, and now we were off to fresh woods and pastures new.

Our train journey from Trieste to Lübeck was remarkable not so much for its route – Villach, Salzburg, Munich, Frankfurt and Hanover – or for its duration of some 36 hours, but more for the make-up of the train itself and for the composition of its passengers. Because the regiment was moving station, many of the soldiers shortly to be demobilised went straight to England, so that there were far fewer to be transported by our train. But this shortage of bipeds was more than compensated for by an excess of quadrupeds. All the horses, hounds, donkeys, dogs and cats that we had been accumulating since the war ended came with us on the train. There were as many improvised stable and kennel trucks as there were passenger carriages. In charge of the latter was the adjutant; of the former, inevitably, Loopy Kennard. It was he, you will recall, who had brought our hounds to Trieste and had run the drag at Basovizia, and he was the 'very age and body' of the cavalry spirit.[1] His nickname, although somehow deserved and fitting, for he was up to any mad-brained trick you could devise, does not give us the complete man. That he was a brilliant and fearless horseman was never in doubt, nor that his performance on skis was such that it was as well not to be on the same mountain; to be driven by him in a car would mean that war, hobgoblins or the devil could hold no terror for you; his outrageous disregard for authority, his eccentricity of method and rejection of orthodoxy were celebrated. Yet behind this outward 'loopiness' is a character at once loyal, steadfast and shrewd, and although his handling of two-legged mares has perhaps been less sure than those of the four-legged variety, there are none of us calling ourselves his friend who are not proud to do so. He has that priceless gift of making the young feel capable of ever-growing accomplishments. To follow him out drag-hunting – as, having been appointed one of his whippers-in, I well knew – was to reach fresh heights of enjoyment in riding to hounds. Needless to say, during our train journey, the horses and hounds were better looked after than the human passengers.

There is perhaps room for one more story about our pack of draghounds before we leave them. Soon after we had settled down in Germany, it was decreed by higher command that there was to be a military tattoo that summer at the Olympic Stadium in Berlin. It was to be a grand affair – massed bands, colourful uniforms, demonstrations of precise drill, physical training displays, and, most important, the horses! One regiment was to perform a musical ride; another, deploying Lancers in full fig, would gallop to the rescue of distressed gentlefolk whose coach had been held up by highwaymen; a third – our own – was to be a hunting scene with the star players, of course, our own draghounds. Getting to Berlin involved another bizarre train journey with some twenty horses, eight couple of hounds – including my three dear bitches, Thankful, Vital

---

[1] In his autobiography, *Loopy* (Leo Cooper, 1990), Sir George Kennard presents his case with wit, elegance and modesty.

and Sapphire, who were becoming world beaters in train journeys – a phaeton for the squire and his lady, saddles, bridles, rugs and other horse furniture, our blacksmith properly equipped, ourselves, not forgetting grooms, regimental wives, friends, children, *and*, to bring some good order and military discipline to this almost unmanageable mob, the Regimental Sergeant Major, Chesty Read, one of the finest rough-riding instructors ever turned out by the Cavalry School at Weedon.

The Last Fence

Once in Berlin there were briefings, rehearsals, getting the timing of leaving barracks so as to arrive at the stadium shortly before our act exactly right, a dress rehearsal, commentary properly translated for the benefit of the thousands of Berliners who would attend, and so on until the grand opening to be honoured by our Commander-in-Chief and the Mayor of Berlin. In order to portray as many aspects of the sport as possible in a mere ten minutes, we had telescoped events severely. As the flood lighting came on, there would be revealed in the arena's centre

Loopy and his hounds with the whips keeping them in a disciplined group. The buttons of our hunting coats gleamed, breeches snow white, boots well polished, hunting caps well brushed – in short worthy of our beautifully groomed horses. Then, in groups, appeared members of the hunt, walking or trotting up, saluting the Master and positioning themselves nearby, some of the grooms, suitably liveried, would walk on bearing silver salvers loaded with stirrup cups, just as the squire and his lady dashed up in the phaeton. Courteous cap-raising, obsequious forelock-tugging would precede the rapid emptying of stirrup cups and their collection; a note on the horn would indicate that it was time to move off, and then – with the floodlights switching to another part of the arena – Loopy's horn would give us the 'gone away', and he would lead his hounds over three well-spaced brush fences, whips and field following, the squire roaring approval as we all galloped out of the arena. After our ten-minute appearance on stage, the half-hour hack back to barracks cooled us down, before supper and a night-club finished off our Thespian evening. So it went on for a week, playing to packed houses, for admission was free, and we all felt the fascination of the boards, while horses and hounds alike entered into the spirit of the thing.

After this, life back in barracks at Lübeck seemed a little thin, but once the hunting season started again, we had some marvellous runs with the hounds, sometimes as far afield as Schleswig or Kiel where other cavalry and horse artillery regiments would act as hosts. Once more we savoured the force of Wilfrid Scawen Blunt's lines:

> To-day, all day, I rode upon the Down,
> With hounds and horsemen, a brave company.

And as Dorian Williams, himself an MFH *and* an ardent Shakespearian, has put it, the horse has always inspired the artist, whether in cave drawings, sculpture, paintings, poetry or prose. So too has the hunting field.

9

Hosses, Dawgs, and Men[1]

What do we, as a nation, care about books? How much do
you think we spend altogether on our libraries, public or
private, as compared with what we spend on our horses?

John Ruskin

In my prologue I suggested that Peter Beckford was mistaken in his
contention that hunting is a dull, dry subject to write upon, and I trust
that the foregoing pages have not proved me wrong. Anthony Trollope
would certainly have agreed with me for in his second novel[2] he included
his first hunting chapter, and thereafter managed to bring the hunt into
twenty or more of his stories. 'I have dragged it into many novels,' he
wrote in his *Autobiography*, 'into too many, no doubt – but I have always
felt myself deprived of a legitimate joy when the nature of the tale has not
allowed me a hunting chapter.' It is a joy shared by many who read his

---

[1] 'Nothing like blood, sir, in hosses, dawgs, *and* men.' *Vanity Fair*.
[2] *The Kellys and the O'Kellys.*

novels, and one still to come for those who have not yet done so, for like Max Hastings[3] I have been surprised by the number of people keen on hunting 'who have never fallen under the spell of Surtees and Trollope'. And indeed those who do choose to read about hunting derive not merely the sheer pleasure of seeing 'hosses, dawgs, and men' realistically, humorously and thrillingly portrayed, but may also learn something about the business that they did not know before. What, after all, says Earl Fitzhardinge? That after half a century in the hunting field, he had learnt nothing, except from a practical point of view, beyond what the pages of Somerville had told him as a boy. He is referring, of course, to William Somerville, from whose epic poem, 'The Chase', Beckford so frequently quotes. This is not surprising for not only does he know, as few men did, what he is talking about, but he puts it into sublime, unforgettable language. Although he could not have known it, some of the advice offered by Somerville is admirably suited to those responsible for seeing that their draghounds are up to the mark. Do not, he tells us, have hounds that are either too large or too small, gigantic or pigmy-like, but go for 'hounds of middle size, active and strong' who 'Will better answer all thy various ends, And crown thy pleasing labours with success'. Like Beckford himself, Somerville is eloquent on the need for kennels to be kept in good order:

> O'er all let cleanliness preside; no scraps
> Bestrew the pavement, and no half-pick'd bones,
> To kindle fierce debate, or to disgust
> That nicer sense, on which the sportsman's hope,
> And all his future triumphs, must depend.

While we are talking of kennels, we may touch too on the matter of obedience, for as has been made clear by accounts of days with draghounds given so far, they can be notoriously disobedient. To counter such tendencies, and given that the master who, with a drag, is probably the huntsman too, can find the time to do so, frequent visits to kennels, where hounds can be called over, become used to their names, in short know and understand you, together with exercising them and correcting

---

[3] *Outside Days* (Michael Joseph 1989).

or encouraging them, can be very beneficial. Steadiness in hounds is the great goal to be aimed at. One of the few points on which Beckford does not agree with Somerville is that of scent, for whereas the latter maintains it depends on the air only, the former believes scent depends also on the soil. For those of us concerned with drag-hunting, of course, scent is not a problem, for we so arrange things that it is more often than not breast-high, so that:

> With nostrils opening wide, o'er hill, o'er dale
> The vig'rous hounds pursue, with ev'ry breath
> Inhale the grateful steam, quick pleasures sting
> Their tingling nerves, while they their thanks repay,
> And in triumphant melody confess
> The titillating joy.

Thus Somerville; but the very name makes us conscious of another Somerville, who, with her co-author, Ross, gave us such unforgettable stories of an Irish RM and his adventures in the hunting field.

Those of us who have followed the fortunes of Major Yeates are unlikely to forget the description and performance of his horse, Daniel, in *Put Down One and Carry Two*. Daniel was just the sort of animal we would all want to possess – tough, steady, imperturbable, up to weight, with an infinite store of tolerance and patience, and able to get over any sort of country.

> Daniel stands sixteen hands two inches in his stockings, of which he wears one white one, the rest of his enormous body being of that unlovely bluish-dun colour to which a dark bay horse turns when clipped. His best friend could not deny that he made a noise; his worst enemy was fain to admit that he was glad to hear it in front of him at a nasty place. Someone said that he was like a Settled Religious Faith, and no lesser simile conveys the restful certainty imparted by him. It was annoying, no doubt, to hear people say, after I had accomplished feats of considerable valour, that that horse couldn't make a mistake, and a baby could ride him; but these were mere chasteners, negligible to the possessor of a Settled Religious Faith.

Most of us who have consistently ridden drag-lines with some nasty places

Formidable country in Co. Londonderry

without losing balance or dignity will have been sensible and honest enough to impute our success to the quality of the horse we have been riding rather than to our own horsemanship.

After a long frustrating wait in heavy rain at the edge of hillside cover, with no sign and only a faint sound of hounds, Major Yeates decides to 'go out of this' and persuades Daniel to ascend the bed of a stream which is turning into a flight of stairs, only, on reaching the top, to be cannoned into by Miss Larky M'Rory vainly attempting to control a grey cob, which, having bumped into Daniel's massive stern, rebounds and subsides. Once on the top of the hill and in spite of fog and wind, they make their way forward until confronted by an unattractive obstacle, a bank surmounted by slaty stone slabs, which instantly induced the grey cob to flee at a tangent, while Daniel calmly hopped over the fence without comment. Yeates's relief to have shaken off his companion is but short-lived, for 'once more I heard behind me on the wind cries as of a storm-driven sea-gull, and the grey cob came up under my stirrup, like a runaway steam pinnace laying itself beside a man-o'-war. Miss M'Rory was still in the saddle, but minus reins and stirrup; the wind had again removed her hat, which was following her at full stretch of its string, like a kite'. Incident continues to mount on incident. They come across a loose brown mare – it is the Master's, Flurry Knox's – so Yeates gallantly decides to make his way to offer Knox Daniel to continue with; then Miss M'Rory parts company with the grey cob in trying to jump a pole across a lane; pursuit of the cob is fruitless, so up on Daniel goes Miss M'Rory, with Yeates walking alongside, until he goes lame; he remounts Daniel with his female companion seated behind him on Daniel's broad back, while 'Daniel continued to conduct himself like a gentleman'; so with fog, rain and darkness to assist them they decend the hill until at last Yeates knows where he is, with a pub just round the corner of the road, but even then the adventure is not over. 'We turned the corner, and were immediately struck blind by the twin glare of the lamps of a motor, that lay motionless, as in ambush, at the side of the road. Even the equanimity of Daniel was shattered; he swung to one side, he drifted like a blown leaf, and Miss M'Rory clung to me like a knapsack'. There stands Lady Knox and a moment later Flurry Knox himself appears behind Yeates with a few muddy hounds, and he is riding – the missing grey cob!

It could only happen in Ireland, of course, and only as told by those uniquely creative chroniclers of the hunting world – Somerville and Ross. Trollope's portrait of hunting in Ireland is very different, but in his own style both observant and entertaining. From the very first time he wrote about hunting, he was always able both to give us accurate pictures and to present us with familiar characters and incidents. Every former or present master of draghounds would be envious of the disciplined conduct displayed by the Kelly's Court hounds:

The dogs were collected round the huntsman, behaving themselves, for the most part, with admirable propriety; an occasional yelp from a young hound would now and then prove that the whipper had his eye on them, and would not allow rambling; but the old dogs sat demurely on their haunches, waiting the well-known signal for action. There they sat, as grave as so many senators, with their large heads raised, their heavy lips hanging from each side of their jaws, and their deep, strong chests expanded so as to show fully their bone, muscle, and breeding.

Trollope amuses us with his oft-reiterated point that masters of hounds, although as mild-mannered and as courteous as could be wished when away from the hunting field, can be fierce and tyrannical when conducting affairs in it. Frank O'Kelly, Lord Ballindine 'was, generally speaking, as good natured a man as is often met, but even he got excited and irritable when hunting his own pack. All masters of hounds do. Some one was always too forward, another too near the dogs, a third interfering with the servants, and a fourth making too much noise'. And when it came to an inexperienced horseman making every sort of *faux pas*, culminating in the unforgivable sin of allowing his horse to come down on the haunches of a favourite young hound, his fury and invective know no bounds. Pronouncing the culprit to be a clumsy, ignorant fool, he says he will be greatly obliged 'if you'd do me the honour to stay away another day, and amuse yourself in any other way . . . you're as fit to ride a hunt as you are to do anything else which gentlemen usually do. May I trouble you to make yourself scarce?'

Trollope also emphasises that nice distinction between two classes of men who go out hunting, those who are there essentially for the business of riding, of getting the maximum out of their horses, and those who reduce the amount of riding to the least compatible with seeing what the hounds are up to. And as he ironically observes it is those who are least active who generally know most about the sport. Not only about the sport, but about the country too for they are familiar with every byway, stream and bog; they remain on the eminence until they see which direction hounds are taking; they understand the wind and its likely effect; they don't like galloping and avoid jumping fences if possible; and yet,

> . . . when a hard-riding man is bringing up his two hundred guinea hunter, a minute or two late for the finish, covered with foam, trembling with his exertion, not a breath left in him he'll probably find one of these steady fellows there before him, mounted on a broken-down screw, but as cool and fresh as when he was brought out of the stable.

Such were the injustices of it all. For the drag-hunting man or woman, however, this nice distinction need not apply, for the whole idea of going out drag-hunting in the first place *is* to gallop, to clear fences, to ride their horses in order to get the maximum out of them, and to be among the first

to finish. Yet even he or she, dedicated to riding a drag-line, would be glad of that local knowledge of byways and out-flanking movements if it should come to the point when their own Daniel or Pacifico or Hercules or grey cob decides to refuse a fence and there is a serious danger of being left behind.

Just as Surtees presents us with Soapey Sponge to enliven his portrait gallery of those dedicated to hunting, so Trollope from time to time gives us someone like his Fred Pepper, a young man in his mid-forties who had hunted with a particular pack as long as anyone could remember. Yet no one knew on what he lived or how he paid for his horses. But he was very good at selling them, and as he seemed able to make a horse do anything he wanted it to, and was generous at giving others a lead over tricky places, men would buy them. Moreover there was no show or bluster or boasting about him. He rode carefully and was a safe man in the field. He liked his rubber of whist and was known to make money at cards, yet there was no question of his actually cheating. He was affable. He had even been known

George Denaro with Draghounds of the 1st Battalion, The York and Lancaster Regiment, Co. Londonderry

145

to lend a horse, and so was popular in his way. He was thus not without virtues.

> That he had no adequate means of his own, and that he never earned a penny, that he lived chiefly by gambling, that he had no pursuit in life but pleasure, that he never went inside a church, that he never gave away a shilling, that he was of no use to any human being, and that no one could believe a word he said of himself – these were specks upon his character.

We have all known such men and have generally liked them.

We have also liked horses who understand their business so much better than we do, and if they pull like the mischief, well, so be it. Better that than the futile urging of a beast who, contrary to all the requirements of drag-hunting, is reluctant to jump. An animal called Bonebreaker, lent by Lord Chiltern to Phineas Finn, would have been just the thing for riding a drag-line, for although he had been advised to ride him with the snaffle, he soon realised that Bonebreaker paid little attention to so weak an instrument. He found too that the horse not only knew what he was about, but was determined to have his own way in doing it. The gag rein might be there, but it was not very effectual.

> When a horse puts out what strength he has against a man's arm, a man must put out what strength he has against the horse's mouth. But Bonebreaker was cunning, and had had a gag rein on before. He contracted his lip here, and bent out his jaw there, till he had settled it to his mind, and then went away after his own fashion. He seemed to have a passion for smashing through big, high-grown ox-fences, and by degrees his rider came to feel that if there was nothing worse coming, the fun was not bad.

This feeling that you have not really a will of your own when riding an animal who knows what he or she is about, who goes straight and is in no doubt about who is in charge was precisely my own sentiment during those joint adventures which I have described when partnering Pacifico, Partisan and, in the early days before we were out in front, Bella. And how happy you were if in spite of being *under* command, rather than *in* command, you were among those to finish well, for as Trollope put it: to ride to hounds is very glorious; but to *have* ridden to hounds is more

*The Staff
College Drag*

glorious still, even though at times you may have incurred the wrath of the master for riding too close to them, and his imprecations may have advanced from a mild: *Hold hard*! to the more urgent and violent cries recalled by Peter Beckford: '*I beg, Sir, you will stop your horse – Pray, Sir, stop – God bless you, Sir, stop! – God d–n your blood, Sir, stop your horse!*'

When we talk of these past centuries' followers of the hunt and indeed other field sports, we think also of the sporting prints which depicted them and which, if we are lucky enough, still adorn our walls.

> Through them we are still familiar with the bustle of the galleried inn-yard when the coaches were starting, the young swell seated in the expensive place of honour beside the mail-coachman on the box, the heavy middle-aged men of business well wrapped up on the seats behind, the red-coated guard in rear of all . . . the shooters in their top hats approaching the partridges that their dogs have pointed in the stubble; the spaniels flushing the cock pheasants out of the brushwood; the hardy sportsman wading through ice and snow after geese and wild duck . . . the hounds in full cry, and the career of the red-coated hunt, to whom the countryside, recently enclosed and drained, presents with its new hedges and channelled water courses the cheerful aspect of innumerable jumps.

In reminding us of these things, Trevelyan does much to remind us too of what we may lose if those who threaten this green and pleasant land, who know nothing of the countryside, who have never experienced the joys of rural life, or taken delight in observing wildlife – if these philistines should have any say in what is to happen. This land was and still is lovely. In the past man's work was able to add to nature's beauty, not detract from it. Houses, barns, stables and cottages of farmers blended harmoniously with the countryside itself, assisted by the use of local stone and traditional style. 'The fields, enclosed by hedges of bramble and hawthorn set with tall elms, and the new plantations of oak and beech, were a fair exchange for the bare open fields, the heaths and thickets of an earlier day.' If it could be done then, it can be done now. The benefits of preserving the countryside are infinite, for by doing so you preserve rural beauty, you preserve wild life, you preserve field sports. And herein lies the indisputable case for field sports – insist on keeping them and you ensure the preservation of wildlife, of rural beauty, the countryside itself. Drag-hunting, however much fun it may be, must always be thought of as an offshoot, a subsidiary to hunting itself. But, as we have seen, they do have some features in common.

Peter Beckford maintained that 'hunting is the soul of country life: it gives health to the body, and contentment to the mind; and it is one of the few pleasures that we can enjoy in society, without prejudice either to ourselves or our friends'. Elsewhere in his great work, Beckford argues that country life itself is beneficial to both mind and body, and even goes so far as to quote from Dryden:

> Better to hunt in fields, for health unbought,
> Than fee the doctor for a nauseous draught.
> The wise, for cure, on exercise depend;
> God never made his work, for man to mend.

In this respect we may say that drag-hunting certainly fulfils the requirement of giving health to the body and contentment to the mind. We may even say that *some* of the qualities of the perfect huntsman ascribed to him by Beckford – 'such as a clear head, nice observation, quick apprehension, undaunted courage, strength of constitution, activity of body, a good ear, and a good voice' – may be equally necessary for him or her charged with hunting a pack of draghounds, for these are general attributes demanding no special skills. And of course the draghound huntsman should, again like Beckford's ideal, be sensible and good-tempered, sober, exact, civil and cleanly, a good horseman and a good groom; but there the likeness ends. For the success of a day's drag-hunting depends, first, on careful preparation, to include seeing the farmers, checking the fences, briefing the runner, alerting the repair team; second, on proper execution of what should be an infallible plan – but, as will have been seen from these pages, does not always turn out that way. Once draghounds have been laid on to the line, all the huntsman must do is ride after them, remain in the saddle while negotiating all the fences, get the hounds under control at the check, and repeat the process until the line has been fully run. Passable competence with the hunting horn, valuable assistance from the whips, making quite sure damage is repaired, giving satisfaction to members of the draghunt, and broad administrative grip – and the thing is done.

But when it comes to hunting proper, it is a very different story. In the first place, whereas for a drag the master is very often huntsman too, while this is not unknown in the wider field of hunting, it is customary that the MFH or joint MFHs will employ a professional huntsman. Trollope presents us with the ideal MFH in the person of Lord Chiltern, who 'in his eagerness as a master of hounds had almost abandoned his love of riding'. To do the job properly had become his great study of life and he did it with unbounded energy. 'His huntsman was always well mounted, with two horses; but Lord Chiltern would give up his own to the man and take charge of a weary animal as a common groom when he found that he might thus further the object of the day's sport. He worked as men work only at pleasure. He never missed a day . . . He was constant at his kennel. He was always thinking about it. He devoted his life to the Brake Hounds.'

As for the huntsman, Beckford tells us:

> His voice should be strong and clear; and he should have an eye so quick, as to perceive which of his hounds carries the scent when all are running; and should have so excellent an ear, as always to distinguish the foremost hounds when he does not see them: he should be quiet, patient, and without conceit. Such are the excellencies which constitute a good huntsman: he should not, however, be too fond of displaying them till necessity calls them forth: he should let his hounds alone whilst they *can hunt*, and he should have genius to assist them *when they cannot*.

There is, of course, another consideration which *all* those concerned with hunting have in common – love of and care for horses and hounds. No matter how profound your knowledge of the country, how total your proficiency with the horn, how ready your heart to throw itself over a fence, how dedicated your application of energy – these will avail you little if you do not first ensure that your horse will carry you where you want to go and your hounds will do what you want them to do. For those of the same opinion as Whyte Melville about where their indebtedness for the best of our fun lies, the business of giving our horses and hounds what they so richly deserve – in the way of stabling and kennels, forage and flesh, exercise and grooming, companions, care, and on the days when they give so much fun and pleasure to others, the making-much-of that we hope allows them to understand how deeply appreciative of them we are – this business will be of great importance in the day-to-day programme of

anyone who has undertaken the duties, and the joys, of helping to keep alive the sport of riding to hounds.

Hounds, of course, must be housed in kennels the year round, but not horses. 'After a long and tiresome winter, surely the horse deserves some repose. Let him then enjoy his short-lived liberty; and, as his feet are the parts which suffer most, turn him out into a soft pasture.' With soft ground and a long rest, his limbs will be refreshed, the night airs and morning dews will invigorate him. How well I remember turning Bella out into a splendid field at Minley Manor, with one of the whips' horses to keep her company and minimise the irritation from flies – how she relished it! And how I cherished keeping an eye on her from my room in the Manor.[4] As for the hounds, they too 'should have some time allowed them to recover the strains and bruises of many a chase' and their diet modified. These reflections take me back to my treasured times as an MDH and we might perhaps take one more look at them.

---

[4] In these days Minley Manor was part of the Staff College and for those students and instructors who lived in it was also the Officers' Mess.

10

Drag-hunting – an Epilogue

For twenty minutes the run very much represents a
steeplechase, and only well-mounted men on quick blood
horses can keep the flying pack in sight. Whether you take the
fences as you would swallow a dose of unpalatable medicine,
or – looking at the clouds – fly 'em like a bird in the air;
whether objectionable and nauseous, or pleasurable and
thoroughly enjoyable, the fences must be swept over without
hesitation, or you may as well pull up and take the road or
bridle-way to the first pre-arranged check.

Charles Armstrong

'How would you like to be a master of draghounds?' It was a
question which I had never expected to be put to me. Yet there I
was in my bachelor quarters at Minley Manor, attempting to mark the
exercise of a struggling Staff College student, and there in front of me – it
was all of 40 years ago – was Rollo Pain[1] one of my fellow instructors and

*The Staff
College Drag
'A good finish
on the flat'*

---

[1] Lieutenant-General Sir Rollo Pain, a great cavalryman, 4th/7th Dragoon Guards, and, like his
wife, Denys, always up with the hounds in the hunting field.

Secretary of the Sandhurst Foxhounds and Staff College Drag, posing this very question. I hesitated, unsure of what it would involve, of whether my somewhat limited experience of whipping-in to our former regimental pack of hounds would be adequate, of whether my military duties would permit such extramural activity, but when I voiced these objections they were unceremoniously swept aside. I was, Rollo said, the obvious choice to be Master of the Drag – an unmarried cavalryman, whose relatively undemanding duties at the Staff College would mean that my time was practically my own, and one, moreover, who had served an apprenticeship as whipper-in to the 4th Hussars' pack of draghounds under the mastership of the incomparable Loopy Kennard! Why, declared Rollo, I was made for the job! Refusal was out of the question. Indeed, the perspicacity of the Military Secretary's branch in sending me to Minley Manor at all had been strikingly emphasised. The only question was – how soon could I start taking over from the retiring master? It was now the beginning of February. Hunting would continue until the Easter break at the end of March. There was plenty of time for me to see how it was all done, get to know the various drag-lines and the farmers and landowners over whose country hounds ran, meet the Sandhurst cadets and Pony Club girls who whipped-in and helped with hound exercise, learn the kennel routine, gain the confidence of the kennel-huntsman, Jack, and – most important – have a few days out with the Drag as a member of the field.

I have already described how these first few days went and how infinitely fortunate I was to make the acquaintance – one which became a profound affection for, reliance on and admiration of – of my beautiful mare, Bella. I should add that at first there had been an idea that I would take over from the retiring MDH, Major Robert Ferguson, not only the position of master, but also his brilliantly performing skewbald gelding, who, with Robert on board, would go like the wind after the draghounds and would treat all the fences with the same attitude of joyous determination as Bella herself, But there arose a question about the gelding's soundness and the idea was dropped. It would have been impossible to find anyone more enthusiastic, courteous, knowledgeable and helpful than Robert during the weeks when I gradually took over his duties. In some ways he reminded me of Goldsmith's Mr Hardcastle who loved 'everything that's old; old friends, old times, old manners, old books, old wines'. He always set himself the highest standards of conduct, was devoted to country life, excelled at all field sports, and, as an instructor at Sandhurst, endeavoured to pass on to those cadets lucky enough to be in his company the principles and ideals of his own admirable brand of leadership. Needless to say, he painstakingly guided me in understanding what I would have to do and how to do it, and on the occasions when I rode with him, he set a fine example of how to stay in front, even though, as previously recorded, I was subjected to the rough edge of his tongue on the occasion that Bella thought *her* proper place was in front and threatened to overtake him. It was clear that Robert had won the respect and affection of all those concerned with the Drag – members, farmers, whips, Pony Club, secretary, kennel-huntsman, runners, line organisers, fence repair teams – and it would now be up to me to do the same. Robert and I became and have remained firm friends.

At our final handing-over meeting, Robert gave me the hunting horn that he had inherited from his predecessor – and which of course was later handed to my successor – and I was ready to go. As explained earlier the Staff College Draghounds were kennelled at Camberley with the Sandhurst Foxhounds, for whom there were two Joint Masters, Mick Close, a former IXth Lancer and Peter Holland, 16th/5th Lancers, both excellent, clubbable men, who shared with me the duties of hound exercise, mounted from September to April, on foot during the summer months. I have touched on the vicissitudes of hound exercise already, and sometimes during summer sorties I would enlist the aid of Jack, the kennel-huntsman, in imposing an additional degree of discipline over our 60-odd charges, who were only too ready to make life miserable for any four-legged pets unwise enough to venture forth from their owners' Sandhurst quarters when we were in the vicinity. Jack was a delightful character, small, lithe, devoted to his hounds, knowing not only all their names, but their breeding and parent packs, indefatigable in keeping the kennels sweet, overjoyed when we were flush enough in funds to afford a new hound van, which he kept in enviable order, a great support to me both at meets of the draghounds and in having the worry ready at the end of a line, always cheerful and unendingly patient in assisting me to learn the names, not just of the eight couple of draghounds – which was easy enough – but the entire pack. The Sandhurst Foxhounds would normally meet twice a week; the Staff College Draghounds once – on Wednesday afternoon.

Wednesday afternoons were therefore the ultimate purpose of it all. We would decide a full month in advance which lines were to be run, so that the meet cards could be printed and sent out in good time. Of course, this meant that the line secretaries would have sought and gained permission from the farmers and landowners. Well in advance of the day I would walk the line with the runner, fence builders and sometimes the whippers-in; we would check what wire had to be removed and later replaced; see about the temporary removal of livestock; ensure that there were proper arrangements for parking cars, horse boxes and trailers; and inform the police. Nearer the day Jack and I would decide which hounds would hunt on the day; the Sandhurst cadets available to whip-in would be warned; horse boxes and trailers arranged if we were not hacking to the meet; the hound van checked; the worry ordered. Finally the day arrived. Mr Hogan, the splendid, former Irish Guards servant who looked after me and a bachelor colleague at Minley Manor, would proudly lay out my hunting kit, which he so lovingly cleaned and polished; and after an early and light lunch, I would motor down to the stables to be greeted by Tedbury, Bella's groom, a Life Guardsman, who loved her as much as I did. He would then lead out a beautifully groomed Bella, coat shining, mane and tail plaited, hooves gleaming, saddle and bridle immaculate. Bella and I then inspect one another, and I hope my satisfaction with her is matched by hers with me. Certainly the attention that Hogan has given to my boots, breeches, black hunting coat with green collar, hunting cap and whip has been intended to complement that which Tedbury has devoted to turning Bella out so well. Tedbury gives me a leg up, checks the girth and gives Bella a caressing pat. I slip my hunting horn into the case attached to the saddle, and we move off at a brisk walk to the kennels, which are only a few hundred yards away. It is about 1.45 p.m. and the meet on this occasion is at the kennels for we are doing the line on Barossa Common, where no matter what weather we have had the going is always good. Some of the field are already on parade, more are arriving, and my whippers-in are waiting. I was very fortunate to have such enthusiastic and competent whips as Tom Hickman, Michael and Andrew Festing – the latter renowned for his painting – Sandy Cramsie and Damer Colville. They were all Sandhurst cadets during my time as Master and usually two would come out on drag-hunting days, sometimes reinforced by Pony Club girls.

Jack comes over to have a word with me and give me some bread and biscuits which I stow away in the pocket of my coat. It is 2 o'clock; I nod to Jack and he lets the hounds out. Among them are Flyer and Driver, Grateful and Handsome – six couple in all – and they cluster round me as I throw them a few morsels, while my two whips get round them. The field has assembled, greetings made, it is time to move off. A toot on the horn and Bella stirs – she is always well behaved at the meet – we trot on, the hounds on my offside, with Tom on their other side and Michael behind. The runner has been gone this half hour, and when we have hacked about half a mile from the kennels, we turn into a grassy lane and lay on. Away the hounds stream, I blow the 'gone away' and Bella now takes charge as the first fence is in sight. The Barossa line is over heath-like country with numerous hunter-trial-type fences, mostly post-and-rail, ditches and a few brush, and runs in a large circle with two checks, each of the three legs being roughly a mile and a half. The going is firm and we maintain quite a furious pace, so that the checks are welcome for a breather and a tightening of girths. Bella, who knows the way as well as the hounds do, is clearly enjoying herself, treating the fences like hurdles, implying almost that she had been hoping for something more demanding – I tell her not to be impatient for next week we will be doing the Holyport line which has some formidable ditch-hedge combinations, brooks and massive post-and-rails.

The value of the Barossa line was that if, for any reason – flooding, a change of farm work, a hard frost elsewhere – a previously planned line could not be used, it was rare indeed that we could not, at short notice and to avoid Hunt members' disappointment, switch to Barossa, which was, of course, WD land.

On this occasion, all goes well, no one comes to grief, and Jack is waiting for us with the worry at the final check. I dismount, hand Bella over to Tedbury, who is also there and makes much of her, blow 'the kill' as hounds fiercely share the worry between them; pleasantries are exchanged with members of the field; Jack and Tedbury return to kennels and stable in the van while, having remounted Bella, I point her in the same direction – she knows well enough which way to go – and together with hounds and whips we hack back to kennels. Jack is waiting for them, and, having discussed our next moves, we part – Tom and Michael returning to the Sandhurst stables, while Bella and I make our way to the 5-star equestrian accommodation and nourishing that Tedbury has made ready for her. There is, you might say, nothing remarkable about our day's drag-hunting, but it has given great enjoyment and satisfaction to many, and the memory of it all is very dear.

Things did not always go so smoothly. Another of our lines on WD land was at Tweseldown, near Aldershot, where there was both a steeplechase course, with a field containing schooling fences nearby, and an excellent hunter trial course, regularly used for an Army event. On the first occasion of my being in charge of the Tweseldown line, Bella – who, unknown to me, had successfully competed in the previous year's Army hunter trial over this same course – took such total control that we completed the first leg in record time, right up with hounds and my arms almost out of their sockets; the second leg included the field with the steeplechase schooling fences, which induced Bella to assume she was winning the Grand National, and it took me some time to re-assume command of hounds at the end of this leg, obliging me to express my profound apologies to impatiently waiting members of the field. The final leg was conducted at a more sober pace, even Bella having taken a lot out of herself after so furious a gallop.

Of course, we all preferred the lines which ran over good farming country with solid fences, including water, big timber and tricky obstacles into or out of woods. I remember one such fence on, as I recall, the Dogmersfield line, which one had to negotiate from a largish field – it was a high post-and-rail and into a darkened strip of wood with an immediate sharp turn to the left. Even Bella was a little circumspect as we approached it, the hounds being well into the wood by this time. But she took it cleverly, at a slight angle, and although I was not as firm in the saddle as I would have liked, collected herself well and made off down the track towards another edge of the wood where an easier fence led us out to a stubble field. Shortly after this was a check, and Bella's boldness and skill were once more underlined, for it was a good twenty minutes before we were joined by any of the field.

It was Bella who made my season as Master at once so rewarding and so relatively free of worry, for it was her combination of gentleness and boldness, of reliability and staying power, of discipline and playfulness, above all of sheer love of hounds and hunting, determination to be in front, and that nobility of heart to overcome all obstacles, however formidable, that made her the perfect partner for a master of draghounds. There is one footnote to her history. During the summer following my season, it became clear that my next appointment would be in London. I reluctantly had to relinquish the mastership, and then the problem of Bella's future had to be settled. Watching her from my window while she was out to grass, I had observed that in the field adjoining hers a farmer kept a mare and foal. The sight of the foal clearly roused in Bella all her hitherto unfulfilled motherly instincts. She would gallop excitedly round the field, neighing loudly, and eventually she jumped an extremely wide ha-ha in order to inspect the foal more closely. This made up my mind. Bella was getting on. We had better not leave it too late. She went to my fellow Master, Mick Close, who knew her well and would give her a happy home. Soon afterwards Bella was in foal herself. Her first filly was named Isabella, and, it is pleasing to recall that, when in turn Isabella had a foal, it went to Pat Sutton, longtime Master of the Staff College Drag, President of the MDH Association, and of infinite help to me in writing this book. It is also agreeable to recall that during my time as Master, the wife of a colleague painted Bella, and in a place of honour at home hangs her portrait.

Apart from Bella, of course, the great pleasure I derived from drag-hunting was owed to many others, indeed all those who had supported the drag – farmers, line secretaries, runners, whippers-in, hunt members and supporters, Jack, Tedbury, Hogan, administrative staff, fence repair teams *and* the draghounds themselves. A Staff College Regulation of 1885 stated that during the winter months the drag was the principal form of

recreation. This may no longer be so, but drag-hunting thrives countrywide and to it many of those who love horses and hounds owe the best of their fun. However much fun it is, though, it can never be a substitute for the real thing, and should never form part of an argument for doing away with fox-hunting.

The Drag![2]

The fire of the year has burnt low in its 'embers',
The farmer has gathered the last of the corn;
'Tis pleasant to find that one's hunter remembers
The cry of the hound and the twang of the horn.

All Melton the fox over pastures may follow!
All London may ride in the road with the stag!
All Brighton hunt hare – up hill – down hollow – !
But give me the devil's delight of the DRAG!!

We're sure of a find and a country most proper,
And pace like a race from the start to the kill;
'Jack Someone' is sure of a curious cropper,
'Tom Somebody else' of a sweet little spill!

Then give a 'clipper' in tiptop condition –
To lick any luxury this will I back,
For twenty short minutes the pride of position
Of first in the field with the garrison pack!

A health – 'To the herring we owe such a lot to –'
In bumpers will help you to swallow my song;
Take that for a toast, and take this for a motto,
'Sit down in your saddles and send them along!'

[2] From the *Household Brigade Journal* 1870.

Appendix 1
Draghounds

By Charles Armstrong

(An extract from *British Hunting*, edited and compiled for
The Sportsman by Arthur W. Coaten.)

This class of hunting differs materially from the pursuit of any animal, inasmuch as the course is previously mapped out, on the principle of a steeplechase, but a wild animal runs anywhere, generally preferring forest or woodland haunts unfrequented by men. If thereby unable to shake off her pursuers, the hare will outrage her natural habits by seeking protection in the rabbit burrow; the weary fox will hide in the pig-stye, utterly regardless of a savage old sow; and the hard-pressed stag will jump into the drawing-room window, or into any similar opening, equally regardless of the party in occupation.

Nothing of this sort occurs in drag-hunting, a description of which here follows. The foundation and formation of the drag-hunt is usually either initiated by the officers of a garrison, who naturally require some diversion during an occasional dull and almost suicidal winter afternoon; or it is started and supported by professional and commercial gentlemen whose important morning engagements debar them from the enjoyment of fox or stag-hunting, and leave them to choose between a gallop with drag-hounds or no cross-country ride whatever.

The former include such drag-hunts as the HOUSEHOLD BRIGADE, which was started in 1863 by Lord Garlies, with two days a week from kennels near Windsor, the present Master being Lord Richard Wellesley, and the amateur whips the Hon. R. C. Lloyd-Mostyn and Mr. H. Thorne.

Of the latter class is the MIDDLESEX FARMERS' Drag-hunt, which was established in 1887, but since 1895 Mr. A. E. Gostling, M.R.C.V.S., has been both Master and huntsman, and he is now one of the hardest riders among London sportsmen.

Old sportsmen will remember that previous to about 1890 the Royal Staghounds hunted that famous shire-like expanse of pasture known as the Harrow country. On the repeated objections of the farmers, the Earl of Coventry discontinued stag-hunting in the hay country of Harrow, and, driven more frequently to the unattractive Windsor Forest, and wired up elsewhere, the Royal Hunt no longer attracted train loads of horses and hunting men from town. Hence came an opening not only for the Middlesex Farmers', but also for the Collindale Draghounds, both of which showed fine gallops on the northern side of London. The latter was discontinued about 1900, but some of the runs remain as fresh as ever in the memory of the writer.

There are various methods of managing a drag-hunt, one of the most popular being as follows. The Master of Hounds usually receives invitations from farmers, who are sportsmen at heart, and they often propose a Hunt breakfast at the farm-house, and offer a fine line of pasture, well adapted for a drag-hunt. The Master, or his representative, inspects the proposed line, and obtains the assent of each farmer throughout the various parishes.

At the kennels may be kept a fox, or a badger, or both, and their excreta are rolled up in a bit of rough sacking, which forms a bundle about a foot long, four inches wide, and two inches thick. This bundle is first saturated with paraffin, and a few drops of oil of aniseed give such pungent nasal flavour as is most exciting to hounds. Aniseed is not a seed, but a fruit. The chemist's shop contains certain expensive oils which are even more maddening to hounds. With a cord about ten feet in length, a man, starting about an hour before hounds, trails this bundle along the firm, scent-holding "billowy grass," occasionally refreshing the bundle by a few drops of aniseed from a pocket flask or vial. Then at about 2 p.m. the run usually commences, the pace being sufficient to spreadeagle all that part of the field which lacks in horsemanship.

Foxhounds drafted from superior kennels are eagerly picked up at low figures for a drag, as in this form of sport they are unable to indulge in the fault for which they were drafted. For instance, a 'skirter' declines to work with others, but jealously desiring independent action, he flies off at a tangent and watching, like a cunning greyhound, for the turn towards him, he then joyfully takes up the running, and for the time being he drives as hard as half a pack. But this independent action is not conducive to the success of the body of the hounds: hence his expulsion from any good foxhound kennel. This hound might become a good drag-hunter as the scent is so powerful that it keeps him on the line, and the direction is usually so straight away that his objectionable habit could not be successfully practised. For twenty minutes the run very much represents a steeplechase, and only well-mounted men on quick blood horses can keep the flying pack in sight. Whether you take the fences as you would swallow a dose of unpalatable medicine, or – looking at the clouds – fly 'em like a bird in the air; whether objectionable and nauseous, or pleasurable and thoroughly enjoyable, the fences must be swept over without hesitation, or you may as well pull up and take the road or bridle-way to the first pre-arranged check.

If there happens to be wire in the line, it has been removed for the day, but if you attempt such wide parallel riding as is often commendable in fox-hunting, you may fall through the wire, in which only a narrow opening has been made. You must therefore ride the line with determination, or decline altogether. This is comparable to the fashionable card game of Bridge, in which you call high when strong enough to fight, and low with a weak hand; or possibly more like giving battle when strong, and retiring when not equal to the occasion. Some second horses are sent on to the check, and the panting steeds which have so gallantly done their work are then either sent home or kept for perhaps another third of the entire run of twelve or fifteen miles. The gallop throughout is a brilliant ride, often over a big country, with hard, unyielding timbers, and yawning brooks, and other formidable obstacles, that tail off the large majority.

Caesar was not more picturesquely brief than the drag-hunter who summed up a rare run with: "The hounds ran like h–l, and the old mare carried me like ile."

Sometimes a circular course is arranged, but it is so large that riders do not notice that they are circling back to the starting point, where the farmer's hospitable table is groaning with luxuries. The usual number of hounds pulled out may not exceed ten couple, whereas fox-hunts frequently use 18½ couple and stag-hunts 15½. No class of hunting can be so successfully conducted with so few hounds, the reason being that hounds never have the trouble of puzzling out the line. The Aldershot Drag has 14 couple in kennel, the Royal Artillery (Woolwich) 15 couple, the Banstead 11 couple, the Essex 14, the Greenford 12, the Household Brigade 15, the Middlesex Farmers' 15, the Shorncliffe 12½, the Staff College 16, Mr. Walwyn's 15, and the Woolmer 18 couple of doghounds. Hounds are always mentioned in couples, and there is a superstition that odd numbers ensure success; thus 18½ or 19½ are usually pulled out for a fox, but perhaps only 8½ for a drag. The Newmarket Draghounds, which provide sport for the trainers and jockeys at the headquarters of the Turf, are under the Mastership of Mr. Kempton Cannon, who rode St. Amant to victory in the Derby.

A drag-hunt may last only one and a half hours, but it is not cheap hunting, because it severely taxes the horses, and the subscriptions are sometimes not less than for the membership of a woodland fox-hunt. Such drag-hunts as the Essex have a ten-guinea "sub," but the Middlesex Farmers' Drag-hunt expects twenty guineas. The Greenford is now abolished, the country joining the Middlesex.

Mr. Walter Winans keeps draghounds in Kent, and during each autumn he takes his costly hunting establishment to Belgium, to the delight of the Royalty and nobility who are then on holiday. His superior hunters have won prizes at the Olympia Shows.

The following lines represent the experiences of many drag-hunters, and possibly of some fox-hunters. They might have been written of the Middlesex Master:

'Twas a caution, I vow, but to see the man ride!
O'er the rough and the smooth he went sailing along;
And what providence sent him he took in his stride,
Though the ditches were deep, and the fences were strong!

'Ere they'd run for a mile, there was room in the front,
Such a scatter and squander you never did see!
And I honestly own I'd been out of the hunt,
But the broad of his back was the beacon for me;
So I kept him in sight, and was proud of the feat–
This rum 'un to follow, this bad 'un to beat!

Appendix 2

The Oxford and Cambridge Drags

The Oxford Draghounds

In a letter to the author Mr Ashley Brodin, Joint Master, writes;

The Hunt originated in around 1840 at the university itself and was formed to teach the art of hunting to young people studying at the university. It was originally called the Oxford University Draghounds. Traditionally, the student master was appointed annually alongside an outside master who supervised. During the mid-1800s, it was not clear where the hounds were kept. Hunting was, at that time, not organised on a weekly basis but, perhaps, once a month. At the turn of the century, the university somehow affiliated itself to the Whaddon Chase and hounds were kept in the Aylesbury area, as far as we can tell. After the Second World War, on the amalgamation of the Bicester and Whaddon, hounds were then transferred to the Straton Audley kennels where they are kept to this day. Unfortunately, as the years have gone by, there has been little interest from the students and I think the last student master was in 1987/88. Since then, we have had no support from the university whatsoever.[1]

One further point of interest is that there was an annual meet at Highgrove prior to HRH Prince Charles's arrival and subsequently we were permitted to hunt in Beaufort country by special invitation. Last year, we had a field in excess of one hundred riders from at least eighteen packs from around the country.[2]

[1] In a further letter, however, Mr Brodin gives the welcome news that undergraduate interest in the draghounds is reviving,
[2] See pages 63–67 for Lin Jenkins's account of a drag hunt at Highgrove in December 1997.

The Oxford Draghounds card is headed: 'We chase nothing, catch nothing, end with nothing, and like to finish where we started'. Its rules are: (i) no one to overtake the Field Master[3]; (ii) anyone stopping must go to the back of the field; (iii) fences must be jumped between markers; (iv) correct riding attire must be worn. The point is also made that farmers and their families over whose land the hunt goes pay no cap on the day.

Cambridge University Drag Hunt

This piece has been produced from information provided by the CUDH and sent to Pat Sutton who passed it on to me. Mr Andrew Lyndon-Skeggs, a former Master of the CUDH and senior Trustee, has also been most helpful in giving me further information. After his Mastership, 1968-70, he produced a book about the Hunt which has been much in use as a guide for subsequent Masters. Mr Lyndon-Skeggs has also generously provided transparencies of CUDH pictures by Lionel Edwards and John King which appear in the book

The Cambridge University Drag Hunt is the oldest existing drag hunt.[4] It is run by undergraduates at the University and therefore Masters change frequently. At present (1998) the Joint Masters are Miss Jennifer Harbison, Newnham College, and Miss Jane Walker, Sidney Sussex College.

The Hunt dates from 1855 when kennels were in Cherry Hinton, providing continuous sport until 1938. In 1946 Mr N.E.C. Sherwood revived the Drag Hunt after Lady Dorothy Bruntisfield's appeal raised funds for new kennels. The hounds are now kept with the Trinity Foot Beagles, another student run pack, at Barton. The kennelman, Paul Smith, sometimes hunts with the TFB, having formerly worked at the Fitzwilliam kennels, Milton. He started with us in 1994. The horses are stabled with Henry Hill at Great Gidding, who is invaluable to the running and continuity of the CUDH. His son, Stephen, a farrier, has whipped-in since 1993 and became Huntsman in 1998. Henry Hill will also provide hirelings.

[3] Easier said than done – see page 28.
[4] A point disputed by dignitaries of the Oxford Draghounds, whose entry in *Baily's Hunting Directory* claims that 'records of the Oxford University Draghounds can be traced as far back as the first part of the 19th century'.

The CUDH has had many distinguished Masters, many of whom have since become noted MFHs. Subscriptions are mostly from the local community or from areas of the meets. About a dozen undergraduates hunt with us regularly, rather a change from former days when the field was mainly made up of undergraduates. The country is hunted by invitation of the Quorn, Belvoir, Cambrideshire, Puckeridge, Fitzwilliam, Oakley, Norfolk Harriers, Fernie, Cottesmore, East Essex and Woodland Pytchley. We are also invited to hunt in Scotland at the end of our season. This annual tour started when Lord Lovat asked us to hunt in Inverness. We still hunt in Fyfe and Duke of Buccleuch's country. The Masters may also take their hounds to their homes during the Christmas vacations. We have visited Crawley and Horsham country and the CUDH have been as far south as Devon.

The lines vary dramatically with location and some country provides very large fences. Bigger days are expensive and are marked with asterisks on the meet card. Obstacles include hedges, dykes and timber. Fields vary from 10 to 100.

The Hunt dress is green with a white collar, and evening dress is the CUDH coat – green, white facings, dark blue collar and buff waistcoat – which may be worn by Masters and Whippers-in. At Whatton House the first part of the line starts with a leap from the ha-ha. In Scotland we once hunted in six inches of snow. Hounds ran extremely well, although we only kept up with them by following their footprints and the marks of the drag.

Our point-to-point is at Cottenham and the course there is also used for point-to-points of Cambridge University and a United Hunts Club event. This last one is run by the CUDH, Cambridgeshire Harriers, the Fitzwilliam (Milton) Hunt and the Trinity Foot Beagles. One of our trustees, Cathy Scott, a former Master, helps the Cottenham Committee to run the CUDH point-to-point.

We have many dinners: Christmas; Panthers'; and a Hunt Ball. These events are often held in Colleges of Cambridge University, and sometimes in the Trinity Foot pub just outside the town.

Ten couple of hounds are drafted to us, mainly from the Fitzwilliam but also from the Oakley, Puckeridge, Woodland Pytchley and Cambridgeshire. Recently we have had a very good Welsh, hairy hound called Fantail. The hounds hunt an aniseed scent, normally dragged by an athletic undergraduate. Formerly it consisted of panther's urine, bought from London Zoo. Hence the runners are still called Panthers.

The continuity of the Cambridge University Drag Hunt is overseen by the three trustees: Andrew Lyndon-Skeggs, Anthony Pemberton and Cathy Scott, all former Masters of the Hunt.

Appendix 3
The Staff College Draghounds

A good deal has already been said about the Staff College Drag in the preceding pages, and of course an account of a day's drag-hunting with one particular pack does not greatly vary from that with another. But to recall once more how some things do not change over the years, and others do, here are a few extracts from the admirably comprehensive archives which are still housed at the Staff College:

Hound Race 1903: Here again we have a reminder of Peter Beckford's observation that his friend would like to see his hounds run a trail-scent and of Lin Jenkins's reference to foxhound contests as one hunt competed with another. Here is the notice which heralded such a contest in April 1903:

The Staff College Drag

169

A Hunting Horn presented by Staff College Drag Hunt will be competed for by 3 Couple of Hounds from each of the following packs –

Household Brigade   WINDSOR
Royal Artillery   WOOLWICH
Shorncliffe   SHORNCLIFFE
Staff College   CAMBERLEY

Race to take place at EASTHAMPSTEAD[1] on April 6th at 3pm. Meet at North Lodge, Easthampstead

Judges:

Sir Robert Wilmot Bt MSH
Mr Frank Goodall

A line will be laid by each Runner if the Master so wishes. The Masters may assist the Judges but must leave the hounds entirely alone to run the line.

Horses will not be allowed inside the park except those of hunt servants.

The first three Couple of Hounds to make marks

1st Hound   6 etc

The pack making most marks to win.

Just as the Household Brigade Draghounds' activities and those of the Royal Artillery were painstakingly and vividly recorded in hunt diaries by those responsible, so were those of the Staff College Drag. Here are two brief records from the early part of this century:

1905 March 4th: Meet at Plough & Harrow, Warfield. Hounds rioted on the way to the covert.[2] We were going to draw as two hares got up right under their

---

[1] The Easthampstead line was still in use in my day as Master.
[2] See page 40 for my own comparable difficulty.

170

noses. However we soon got away and ran past Warfield Hall, and then on over Jealott's Hill and checked on the Hawthorn Hill Race Course[3]. Laid on again just below Mr Cunard's house and ran on over the Race Course; and then leaving Cokely Bridge on our right, down Holloway Lane to Cabbage Hill where we finished. There was a small field but a good many strangers. Took out 11½ couple of hounds. Everyone agreed that this was the best line we have had yet.

1905 October 24th: Easthampstead East Lodge. Ran past the Home Farm, the back of Mr Burwick's house, through the White Gates and intended to cross 'the Big Fence' in the bottom, but the line was by mistake laid the other side of

Hunt Staff and Hounds, Staff College Drag 1935/6

[3] Hawthorn Hill was frequently part of the Household Brigade's drag-lines, and was still very much in use in my day, as was also Cabbage Hill.

the little copse and took us into the road over an awkward rail which caused some 'alarm and despondency' but no casualties (except to the rail), then on nearly to Holmes Green and right handed to Lock's Farm. Laid on again in front of the house, and ran the usual line over the Tangley Brook to Wokingham Pumping Station. A field of about 40 was out.

These events of nearly a hundred years ago could just as easily have taken place and been similarly recorded today. Another enduring and very well liked annual event is the Farmers' Dinner. For the years 1903, 1904 and 1905, the lovingly produced menu card shows the Master (and huntsman) in hunting kit of 1870 – the year the Staff College Drag Hunt was established – sitting at a table on which rest hunting cap, whip and decanter, declaiming:

> Confound your Water!
> give us the wine, and let's
> have a toast;
> What say you to
> (drag)-hunting'!

Appendix 4

The Drag Hunt

The Staff College Drag is, during the winter months, the principal form of recreation
(SC Regulations 1885)

Founded in 1871 by Captain the Honourable Heneage Legge, Coldstream Guards who later commanded the 9th Lancers. The original committee consisted of:

Captain the Hon H. Legge, Coldstream Guards   – Master
Captain G. S. Schwabe, 6th Dragoon Guards
Captain C. F. Colville, 54th Regiment
Captain R. L. Leir, 31st Regiment   – Whipper-in
Lieutenant H. B. Walmsley, 56th Regiment

Captain Legge crashed at his first educational fence (probationary examination) and was succeeded as Master by Captain Leir who hunted the hounds for ten seasons – 'never was there a keener or more energetic master'. The pack was eighteen couple of dog hounds – a mixed one was

Hunt Staff and Hounds, Staff College Drag 1935/6

173

found too much nuisance as they were always fighting and one of them, Bellman, appeared in a play at Drury Lane.

> The Hound that once through Drury Lane
> The fame of hunting spread
> Now rushed away with music gay,
> And filled us all with dread.

Captain Leir handed over the horn to Lt Col H. M. Manvers Moorson RA in 1882 and was presented by 101 officers with a Mentieth bowl and two tall flagons to enable him to drink 'The Drag for Ever'.

Captain (later General Sir) H. L. Smith-Dorrien became Master in 1887 and was responsible for the first Staff College steeplechase under Grand National Hunt Rules, replacing the point-to-point introduced by Captain Leir. Smith-Dorrien considered the Drag 'as quite the most important part of the curriculum'.

Rumour had it that those who did not go hard with the Drag stood little chance of a staff job. Captain (later Lieutenant-General Sir) Spencer Ewart disagreed and proclaimed, 'I am a Highlander and always have been a Highlander. I hate the sight of a horse and absolutely refuse to bow down to the tyranny of a horse.' However, subsequent masters included Allenby, Hunter-Weston, Godley and Hubert Gough.

The Drag was disbanded during the closure of the college 1899–1900 but was set going again in 1901 by a grant of £200 obtained from the Treasury by General Sir Evelyn Wood the Adjutant-General who considered that 'the most gifted staff officer is useless in the field unless at home in the saddle'.

Royal Navy students joined the college in May 1906 and 'steered their mounts with the Drag with an intrepidity as amazing as it is destructive'.

The college was again closed from 1914–18 but following Evelyn Wood's hardly won precedent after the Boer War, the War Office gave a grant of £23.10s.6d to assist in the re-establishment of the Drag under Major M. Graham, 16th Lancers in 1919.

The Farmers' Dinner was established in 1924 and was held in the Rawlinson Hall and an annual cricket match was held later.

The departure of the horse from the Army dealt the Drag a severe blow. After the Second World War the Treasury was in no mood to be generous but in 1947 the pack was reformed jointly with the Royal Military Academy. It still exists but is no longer considered the most important part of the curriculum, although no one has suggested that it is detrimental to an officer's career.

There is in the Staff College Drag Hunt archives such a wealth of material that justice can hardly be done to it in a few pages – account books, hunt diaries, lists of hounds, scrap books with innumerable photographs, details of point-to-points, Farmers' Dinners, Hunt committee meetings, the various drag-lines and their characteristics, names of landowners and farmers, names of members – all recorded with the same loving attention to detail and accuracy as those of the Royal Artillery and Household Brigade Drag Hunts. Two further nuggets of information may command our attention here:

Finance 1931-32: In round figures expenditure was as follows:

Buildings	£133	Hound Purchase	£22
Car	75	Hedging &	
Clothing	25	Fencing	33
Compensation	2	Management	78
Fuel	33	Subs & Tips	35
Hound		Tools	13
Maintenance	235	Veterinary	37
Insurance	7	Wages	297

It is pleasing to observe that the principal sums are those concerned with the hounds and those who looked after them and the horses.

Drag Lines 1980–81: When in 1963 it was sensibly decided that the Sandhurst Foxhounds would join the Bisley Foxhounds as a separate civilian Hunt, it was possible to concentrate the Sandhurst and Staff College activities on the Drag, and as a result a number of formerly lapsed drag-lines were revived and more acquired. This meant that, by 1980–81, the Staff College and Royal Military Academy Sandhurst Draghounds had no fewer than fifteen lines – Allanbay Park, Bramshill, Chawton, Eversley, Liphook, Mapledurwell, Minley, Moundsmere Manor, Rotherfield Park, Sherfield on Lodden, Shottesbrooke Park, Staff College (i.e. Barossa

Common), Tweseldown, Winkfield, Wokingham. With such a wealth of country and with the splendid support that the Drag enjoys from all those concerned, it is small wonder that it continues to thrive.

'Long live the Drag' for 'the Drag never dies!'. These words are taken from the 1896 Hunt diary, and the extracts from it which follow show that little has changed a hundred years on.

Tuesday, January 28th, 1896.

FIRST LINE. Evendon's Farm to Barkham Rectory. A field of some forty riders assembled to run what was expected to be a 'rotten' line, but which turned out to be a most enjoyable one. The line ran north of Barkham Church, sharp to the left, west of the church over the road, down to the brook in the meadows near Barkham Square, then right-handed over the road again, the second time over the brook and up to the Rectory.

'Cheap at five & twenty bob!'

Very early in the run the junior Junior lost his hireling and did capital

time on his own legs for the rest of the line.

Captain Findlay seemed to prefer jumping into the brook rather than over it, and administered a drenching to one or two interested onlookers, whose keenness overcame their discretion.

The second line ran from the 'Bramshill Hunt' P.H. over the road, due south to West Court, where Mr. Buchanan very kindly provided tea, drinks and a gallery of some twenty ladies; the latter took up a position flanking the last fence over which the field came in a long extended line, among them the junior Junior again on his own legs, a means of locomotion he is apparently partial to. Our Major was amongst the last arrivals, having stopped *en route* to rub his nose in the mud. On arrival he was the subject of much sympathy of the fair, whom alone the brave deserve.

This evening, a Staff College Officer, dining in Berkshire, was a participant in the following conversation: –

She (whom he took in to dinner): 'I saw the Staff College drag to-day, I never saw such a rag-tag and bob-tailed assemblage in my life, such poor riders, too!'

He: 'Yes. Not much of a lot, are they?'

She: 'No! Awful bounders!'

He: 'Yes – er, I am one of them.'

Confusion and dismay on the part of the fair one.

Thursday, March 5th, 1896.

THE Draghounds met to-day, because of the Grand Military Meet. Bean Oak Farm, near Buckhurst. A large field.

The line was a capital one with every variety of jumps. It ran N.E., then to the left up to Billingbear E. Lodge, sharp left again over the sunken fence, to finish in the next field.

Refusals, as usual, commenced early. One bold fencer put his rider down, and, hurrying on, gave the field an exhibition of his lepping powers. This gave H. E. W. a rare opportunity of showing of what mettle, or shall we say 'metal,' he was made.

By dint of much shouting he gets a yokel to stop the runaway, swops mounts, and sends his own (a slow mover) to the downcast hero, with a message that 'he'd wait for him at the finish.'

The language which this kindly message evoked brought back to many of us tender reminiscences of sketching on horseback.

The sunken fence puzzled several of the horses. One made for an adjacent gate, deposited his rider over it, stopping himself behind to view the performances of his fellow quadrupeds. The rider followed his example, standing for a few seconds on his head for the purpose. Almost all those who slowed before the jump failed to negotiate it. Even Bramley had a fall. C—b, who was out as a spectator, kindly volunteered to give the refusers a " lead," unfortunately he hadn't previously consulted his horse on the subject and the latter proved contrary. C—b to avoid a scene wisely gave in and retired to the gate.

The second line was as good as the first, and there were no casualties, though refusing was the order of the day. De T was a bit off jumping, and seemed bent on forcing other horses to follow his example by crossing them at the jumps. Two head dresses, a hat and a Crammer boy's cap, besides several odd spurs, were lost on the course, and are now advertised for. We hear Willoughby is offering excellent prices for part worn pairs of the latter.

Saturday, March 28th, 1896.

THE FARMERS' DINNER.

AT 5.15 p.m. to the minute the two brakes and a dogcart were filled, the roll was called, the twenty-four volunteers for the Farmers' Dinner were reported present, the word was given and off we started for Wokingham. We could not fail to be struck by the retiring nature and the extraordinary good manners of the Senior Division, no doubt the result of sixteen months at the S.C. Were they the men to take advantage of their superior age, learning and respectability to push themselves forward, to refuse to be left at home and perhaps to disappoint some of their younger brethren who were looking forward to an evening of intense enjoyment? Quite the contrary! With the exception of the Hunt Officials, who could hardly be expected to stand aside, only one Senior so far forgot himself as to insist upon his right to be present at the jovial gathering.

The conduct of these Voluntary Cinderellas is all the more praiseworthy when we remember that a notice to the effect that there would be no dinner that night at the Staff College had been for some days on the notice board. We imagine, however, that emergency rations were called upon, as they did not appear particularly hungry next day. We noticed, with great pleasure, the presence of Captain D. Henderson, A. and S. Highlanders, who had consented to take the part of pianist for the evening. He did his work, as always, admirably, and we can confidently recommend him to anyone intending to give a Children's Dance or a Punch and Judy Show as a sober, untiring and most obliging performer. Terms, moderate.

We arrived well before the appointed hour and found our guests assembling in great force. After a brief inspection of the Hall and Table, which would not have disgraced a Royal Banquet, we proceeded to business. Mr. Robinson, the mess man, had provided an excellent spread, and it was done ample justice to. The sweets were extremely popular; one gentleman, who had not given one the idea that he was keeping a lot in hand, disposed of wine jelly, jam tarts, blanc mange, fruit compôte and Californian cream in a way that would have made the ordinary public schoolboy blush for shame. Our Secretary had provided us with an excellent fluid, which we had noticed him sampling about three times a week for the last month, 'just to make sure it was all right, don't you know.' It sparkled and fizzed like anything, was of a beautiful pale canary colour and the bottles were plastered with gold foil. The taste was a trifle peculiar, though not unpleasant, reminding one slightly of some of the liquids we toy with on Saturdays at the Telegraph Course. One could drink any quantity without getting 'forrarder.' Our new master owned two bottles without danger, and we all woke up as fresh as larks.

As soon as the cigars had been passed round, our Chairman, who was evidently in grand form, proposed the usual loyal toasts, which were received as they should be in an assemblage of soldiers and farmers. When the noise had subsided, Furse mounted the platform and gave us 'the Meynell,' and right well it went too.

The programme annexed shows the speakers and the toasts they gave and responded to. They were all good and to the point, and were received in a way that showed unmistakably the friendly feeling which exists, and we trust always will exist between the farmers and the Staff College Drag. Sandy covered himself with glory, his tuneful rendering of 'Cookey' was so appreciated that an 'encore' was absolutely necessary. In his speech he told us how the Commandant had alluded to the Drag Secretary as a mole who works silently and underground, he at the same time assured us of the great affection he had, not only for the farmers, but for their wives. Mr. Sturgess, in proposing the health of the vice-chairman, said he quite agreed as to the 'mole.' The mole was the most voracious, pugnacious, and immoral creature in the world, and it would be a good day for the farmers when they could inform their wives that the reign of a new Secretary had commenced. We are afraid that, considering the charm of our new Secretary, that it is but a case of out of the frying-pan into the fire.

Mr. Lane, Mr. Auckland, and Mr. Wilson were, as usual, most kind in their remarks, they all declared that if the Drag went over their land and they wanted to see which way the hounds had gone they had to take out their best magnifying glasses and examine the turf for crumpled blades of grass, and even then they were not always successful. As for a gap, they had never seen one made, and if there happened to be one in the hedge it must have been the old cow's fault.

Our Chairman called for many songsters, each better than the last. Mr. Cox with 'John Peel' fairly brought the house down. Furse wound up the evening with a few appropriate verses to the tune of "As long as the world goes round." We cannot do better than repeat them here.

Some say that our Staff College Drag must soon end,
That farmers are sickened of fences to mend.
Well! If this is so – which Heaven forefend! –
I wonder how long we shall last?
Why, as long as the world goes round,
While good British farmers are found,
As long as they live
They'll be ready to give
Protection to hunter and hound.

Now Point to Point Races are all very well,
And a horse that can win one is easy to sell,
But when for a week it's been raining like hell,
I wonder how long they will last?
As long as the world goes round,

Will gallant young bloods be found,
Who swear that a fall
Is just nothing at all,
When there's plenty of sop on the ground.

Now what do you think of your dinner to-night?
The fare has been passable, faces are bright,
And I'm glad to say no one seems to be tight,
But I wonder how long this will last?
The longer the wine goes round
The larger your heads will be found,
And I beg you'll take care,
When you rise from your chair,
Or you'll possibly land on the ground

Tuesday, March 31st, 1896.

MEET at Bannister's Farm. Alas! the last day of the season! and such a season! To do honour to the occasion a field of forty-five mustered, all determined to ride hard. A perfect day, rather hot perhaps, with the smell of "them stinking violets" in the air. Hounds are laid on just west of the lane from Bannister's to the farm. A word of warning from the Secretary about a duck pond somewhere, and we are off. Forty yards in front was the first fence, beyond it the fateful pond. On the right, refusing galore; on the left – splash, and three sportsmen are in the pond. They were cadets, and the Easter Holiday is on, so they won't be required for a few days, and we left them there. Next comes the road, the landing boggy and trappy, but no grief. One horse made a fine double, clearing bank and bog first jump, and the opposite bank the next. Out of the road into deep fields. Here the hounds went away from us, but were caught up, and somewhat pressed on the high ground, where the going was capital. The Master, second whip, Bobby Hargreaves, Haig, Wise, and Furse abreast of hounds, the rest closing up. The first whip has a fall early in the run, and is left with a horse without a bridle, or a bridle without a horse, we forget which. Graham's horse gave him a fall, and very nearly a second. De Tomkyn's slithered on to his nose, but got up cleverly. Burrowes arrived with a broken hat, which looked suspicious, and so the first line ended. Rather a crowd at the check in a narrow and dusty road.

THE second line was from Arborfield Cross to Barkham Square. A large field again, heavy going, and much stringing out. After passing Handpost Farm the line swung right-handed down the hill west of Barkham Rectory and then up over the road. At this point a sporting pony in a trap tried to join the line. He got well on to the bank, but the cart wouldn't follow, and the driver got him back with difficulty. The line now swung to the left down a fine grass slope to Barkham Brook, Here there was much refusing, at one time nine horses fighting on the take off bank. One rider, not a S.C. man we hoped, at last dismounted in despair, and begged a spectator to 'ride the damned brute over!'

One more fence and Barkham Square is reached. Here Mrs. Greenfield was at home to the Drag and all the neighbourhood. Having done ourselves nobly, thanked our kind host and hostess, and lighted one of his

1903 Wishing you a Merry Xmas From the Staff College Drag

best cigars, we rode home quietly behind it to congratulate ourselves on having so good a finish to the season.

Never again shall we welcome, as such, our best of Masters, or be shown the way by the cheeriest of whips. Never again will Mac delight our eyes with the sight of his manly form faultlessly attired in the Drag livery. But, no matter, the Drag never dies! Long live the Drag!

This book, devoted as it is to recording the doings of those who hunt with the Drag, would, however, be quite incomplete without a sketch of those who don't.

FINIS.

Appendix 5

Royal Artillery (Bordon) Hounds

The property of the Officers, Royal Artillery,
Bordon 1938–39

Age	Name	Sire	Dam
1933 6 years	PAGEBOY	Quorn Gallant, '28	Duke of Beaufort's Piteous, '29
	WOODMAN	Cattistock Trickster, '27	Their Woodbine, '31
	DOWRY	H.H. Tomboy, '31	Their Dowager, '27
	CHANTRESS	Tedworth W'd'lands Alfred, '29	Their Countess, '29
1934 5 years	CRASHER	H.H. Calendar, '31	Their Handsome, '30
	WOODLAD	Albrighton Regal, '30	Their Wisdom, '30
	PILGRIM PROCTOR }	Surrey Union Prompter, '29	Chiddingfold Prudence, '31

Age	Name	Sire	Dam
	NOVA	H.H. Nathan, '29	Their Woodlark, '31
1935 4 years	RASSELAS	Duke of Beaufort's Premier, '31	His Grace's Rarity, '30
	WEXFORD	Grafton Wildman, '29	Their Garnish, '30
	PLEASANT	Grafton Prancer, '28	Their Wily, '30
	DRUMMER	Chiddingfold Daystar, '30	Their Notable, '31
	RATTLE	South Dorset Goodwood, '32	Cattistock Raiment, '32
	BLATANT BLUEBELL }	Sir E. Currie's Tuner, '27	Cattistock Blackbird, '32
	DISTANCE	Cleveland Ranger, '31	Cattistock Dialect, '31
	GAMESTRESS	Oakley Gordon, '31	H.H. Tenby, '31
1936 3 years	VALET	Bicester Warrant, '31	Their Vanity, '33
	VANDYKE	Bicester Verger, '29	Their Warning, '32

Age	Name	Sire	Dam
	DRAYMAN	S. & W. Wilts Godfrey, '28	Meynell Drastic, '33
	ARTICLE	H. H. Arrogant, '30	Their Charming, '32
	GOLDFINCH	S. & W. Wilts Godfrey, '28	Whaddon Chase Daylight, '32
	BUSHMAN	Whaddon Chase Burglar, '34	S. & W. Wilts Swelter, '33
	LOAFER	N. Hertfordshire Locksmith, '34	Their Noisy, '31
	RUTHLESS	Belvoir Rupert, '30	Their Trilby, '29
	SABLE	Grafton Screamer, '30	Their Tally, '32
	STEADY	Cattistock Brackley, '32	Their Stainless, '34
	WARDEN	H.H. Wildaire, '33	Their Candid, '30
1937 2 years	WANDERER	Hambledon Rally Wood, '32	Silverton Wagtail, '32
	CARDIFF	Old Berks Chanter, '30	Grafton Harpy, '34

Age	Name	Sire	Dam
	SIMPER	Heythrop Student, '29	Grafton Gaiety, '34
	RIFLEMAN	N. Hertfordshire Locksmith, '34	Meynell Ringdove, '32
	BUSTLE	Whaddon Chase Burglar, '34	Brecon Filigree, '35
	TOILET	N. Hertfordshire Locksmith, '34	Their Tempest, '34
	SEARCHER	Belvoir Seeker, '31	Their Seldom, '30
	GRANBY	Belvoir Seeker, '31	Their Greeting, '31
	RAGLAN RACHEL }	Belvoir Richmond, '34	Their Truelove, '33
	REASON	Belvoir Richmond, '34	Their Trespass, '33
	RUSTIC	Cattistock Rallywood, '30	— Ruin, '34
	HARVESTER	R.A. Harrier's Pagan, '34	Their Honesty, '33
	HEARTY	Kilkenny Grasper, '29	S. & W. Wilts. Harriet, '35
	MUSIC	Wilton Stoker, '33	Brecon Music, '32

Age	Name	Sire	Dam
	PIRATE	Blackmore Vale Truant, '33	Their Passive, '34
	VAGABOND	Blackmore Vale Venger, '34	Their Tuneful, '34
1938 1 year	RECTOR RAINBOW RECKLESS }	Rodney, '33	Racket, '32
	TRAVELLER	N. Cotswold Halo, '34	N. Hertfordshire Treaty, '35
	SONGSTER	R.A. Harriers Hotspur, '33	Their Spangle, '35
	LICTOR	Wilton Villager, '34	Their Languid, '35
	NOBLEMAN	Cambridgeshire Noble, '35	Their Handsome, '35
	BARRISTER	Puckeridge Brigand, '34	Cambridgeshire Artful, '35
	DOLPHIN	Cambridgeshire Collier, '33	Their Daylight, '34
	COVENTRY	Cambridgeshire Trimmer, '34	Their Cowslip, '34
	MERLIN	Cambridgeshire Wizard, '36	Their Mercy, '34
	WICKLOW	N. Staffs Warlock, '33	Essex Union Winifred, '33

Appendix 6

Drag-hunting – Advice for Beginners

1. If you want to go out with a pack of draghounds, both you and your horse must be capable of negotiating a cross-country course of between 6 and 10 miles with a variety of up to 40 or 50 fences, some of which will be stiff and may include hedges, ditches, brooks, posts-and-rails, gates, stone walls. The length of drag-lines and the number and nature of fences will vary with particular Hunts. If a line has three parts or legs (some hunts refer to each part as a line), it is customary for there to be a check in between each leg.

2. Drag-hunting is quite different from fox-hunting. The hounds hunt a laid scent over a prepared course which has both natural fences and some specially prepared ones in order to keep damage to a minimum. This means that some of the fences are fairly narrow, as you might expect to find on a hunter trial course. You must always remember that members of a drag hunt are the guests of the farmers and landowners over whose land they ride.

3. If you have never been out with a pack of draghounds before and wish to do so it will be wise to go to the meet with someone who knows all about it and can advise and guide you as to the procedure. Depending on where hounds are meeting, you may be travelling by horse box or trailer, or you may be hacking to the meet. In the former case, you will have ascertained where you may park the vehicle for unboxing and later boxing again. In the latter case you will have worked out how long it will take you to hack from stables to meet. In either case you

will wish to be punctual, that is to be at the meet shortly before the advertised time. You will also wish to ensure that you and your horse are well turned out and we will come to the question of dress later.

4. At the meet itself, which may be in the morning or afternoon, you cannot do better than be quiet and unobtrusive, although, of course, you will wish to greet any friends who may be there. If the horse you are riding should be restive or excited, take it to one side, perhaps accompanied by the friend you may be with, and above all do not impede the hounds or hunt servants. You will find that when the Master appears with his hounds and whippers-in, he will position himself in some central, chosen spot, with the whips getting round the hounds. It is customary for the Master to greet the field by raising his hunting cap, and he will himself – the Master, of course, may be a woman – be similarly greeted. Remember that there may be a number of supporters or followers on foot, who may even follow the dragline as far as they can by Land Rover or other vehicle. If the meet is at someone's house or an officers' mess, there may well be a stirrup cup offered to all those present. If mounted, you will find that the hosts and their helpers will relieve you of your glass before things get underway. Now we come to the actual business of the day.

5. Half an hour or so before the meet, the runner, whose job it is to lay the scent by dragging a bag containing the 'smell' over the pre-arranged course, will have set off, probably in a Land Rover, and having completed his run, laying the scent for the first part of the line will go on by Land Rover to the start of the second leg and, at the appropriate time, again run with his bag over the course, and so on. At the scene of the meet, the Master will have judged that it is time to move off, and having sounded a short note on his hunting horn, will lead off with the hounds, followed by his whippers-in. If the Hunt has a Field Master he or she will probably be the next to move. Not all packs of draghounds do have a Field Master whose job it is to control the field, but a senior, experienced member of the Hunt may well be appointed to do so. After all those mounted have moved off, followers in vehicles or on foot, are free to move too, keeping their distance from the horses and hounds.

6. The Master will then hack to the beginning of the line, and then lay hounds on, that is to say encourage them forward to where the scent has been laid. Hounds will give tongue and stream away, the Master will blow the 'gone away' and will ride after hounds, followed by his whippers-in and the field, who are nominally controlled by the Field Master. But it must be conceded that once things have got this far, you as a member of the field may well find yourself indulging in something closely resembling a point-to-point and sometimes competing with other members for the privilege of being first over the next fence. If your horse is a freely jumping one, steer clear of others as far as you can and let your horse do what he knows best. If, on the other hand, you have a reluctant animal, there is no harm in letting someone else give you a lead, provided you don't impede others. Fields, of course, will vary in number from hunt to hunt. There may be, say, twenty mounted; there may be more, even between 50 and 100 for some special meets, but the procedure will be similar. Some hunts have alternative, easier fences for those who might have trouble at the big ones.

7. After a mile or two of the first part of the line, there will be a check – that is, the runner will have lifted the scent, so that hounds have nothing to hunt. At this point, if all goes well, they will cease hunting the line and mill about uncertainly. It is then the task of the Master and whippers-in to get round the hounds and get them under control. After a pause of perhaps fifteen minutes, the whole process is repeated with the Master moving off to lay on the second leg. You may notice at this point that the fence repair team is in action, dealing with any damage that might have been done.

8. The number of legs and checks will vary with hunts, but, as an average, there will be three parts of the line, each of 2 miles or so, and then, at the end of the final leg, where the kennel-huntsman is likely to be waiting – with the hound van nearby if hounds are returning to kennels by this means – he will have with him the 'worry', usually a large piece of flesh or meat. When the field has arrived – or those who have stayed the course – the Master will dismount, hand his horse to a willing, waiting holder, and, as the kennel-huntsman throws hounds

the worry, which they instantly begin to devour, the Master will blow 'the kill'.

9. This really ends the day, which, dependent on whether all has gone smoothly and the nature of the line and country, plus size of the field, may have lasted an hour and a half from moving off at the meet to the final check. But it is probable that both horses and riders will have been well exercised and will have thoroughly enjoyed themselves. The hounds will be looking forward to a feed back at kennels. Dispersal at the end will vary. If the line has followed a large circle, horse boxes and trailers may be nearby, but whatever the circumstances after exchange of pleasantries, the Master, assisted by whippers-in, will ensure the hounds return safely to kennels, either by hacking back or by hound van, and, of course, the hunt staff will either ride or box their horses back to where they are stabled, ensuring before themselves venturing homeward, that all is well with horses and hounds. The field and other supporters will make their own arrangements, while making sure that no gates are left open and that parking areas are left tidy.

10. Now a few more practical points for those who wish to take up drag-hunting. You will see from the catalogue of Drag Hunts on page 194 that there are sixteen packs of draghounds in Great Britain and the Channel Islands and one in Ireland. This catalogue will show you whom to contact if you wish to become a member or wish to take part as a visitor. It also gives full details of the country hunted over, sometimes the types of fences, amounts of subscription and cap (this last charge is for non-members), on which days hounds meet, where kennels are and so on. You will also find the names of the current hunt staff – joint masters, whippers-in, hon. secretary, kennel-huntsman, point-to-point secretary. There is often a short history of the hunt included, and details of the hunt uniform. You will also find in some cases the names of the chairman, hon. treasurer, supporters club secretary. It is often the case with drag hounds that one of the joint masters also hunts hounds, but sometimes there is an appointed huntsman.

11. As we must assume that you are already a competent horseman or horsewoman, you will certainly be aware that the horse to carry you

surely and safely over a drag-line will cost quite a lot. At the time of writing an average price for a good hunter will be in the region of £5,000, while for junior members it should be reckoned that a pony capable of doing what is needed will not be less than £2,000. So you should be thinking of a price range somewhere in that bracket. And don't forget the point made earlier in the text of this book. If someone trying to sell you a horse or pony tells you he or she will jump anything when he or she wants to, make sure it will also do so when *you* want it to.

12. As for dress, you cannot go wrong if you wear normal hunting kit, i.e. boots (black), breeches, dark hunting coat, stock and regulation hunting cap, string gloves, hunting crop. If you become a valued member of a particular hunt, you may be invited to assume the hunt collar and buttons. But for junior or occasional participants, Pony Club members, etc., jodhpurs and hacking jackets are normally quite acceptable. You will no doubt – or if not, your parents will – be aware of the cost of keeping a horse, whether in your stables at home or at livery. It is not inexpensive, but as Whyte-Melville has told us and as is repeatedly demonstrated in the foregoing pages, the best of your fun, you will freely admit, will be owed to horse and hound.

13. Finally, you will find that those who enjoy and help to organise drag-hunting are an agreeable set of fellows and fillies, and if you turn to them for further advice as to how to go about it, this advice will be forthcoming with the same spirited dash that they themselves display when riding at their fences.

Appendix 7
Draghounds

Great Britain and the Channel Islands

*Note: The * next to the title of a Hunt indicates that it is officially recognised by the Masters of Draghounds and Bloodhounds Association.*

* ANGLESEY

Distinctive Collar: Blue. Evening Dress: Red coat, blue collar.
Jt Masters: (1991) T I Beardsley, Cwyrt Lodge, Maenaddwyn, Llanerchymedd, Holyhead, Anglesey. Tel: 01248 470545; (1991) Trevor Wear, Gors Goch, Llanrhuddlad, Holyhead, Anglesey LL65 4BD.
Hon Sec: (1991) Trevor Wear, Jt Master.
Hon Treasurer: (1997) Mrs S Young, Hiraethog Pennant, Eglwysbach, Colwyn Bay, Clwyd.
Huntsman: Mr I Graves.
Whippers-in: (1993) Mr I Evans; (1997) Miss L Wood.
Kennels: Llain Grin Kennels, Trefor, Holyhead.
Meet: Saturday.
Subscription: Annual £220; five-day £95; Cap £22.
The country lies in the Isle of Anglesey. There is a wide variety of terrain for such a small area (about 20 miles across), from open stone-wall country to bank and ditch and thorn hedges in the woodland areas, though there is a predominance of stone walls. Lines are laid closely simulating a foxhunt. The country is also hunted by the Snowdon Valley foot pack.
The Hunt was formed in 1972–73 by the former Masters and a small group who had previously been travelling to Denbighshire for their hunting. The country had not been hunted by a mounted pack since the

Anglesey Harriers closed kennels at the end of the 1939–40 season. It was started as a drag hunt because of the limitations of the country not having been hunted for over 30 years.

Former Masters: E J O'Donnell, 1979–85, Major & Mrs L G Heysham, 1973–78 and 1985–86, E Roberts, 1986–91.

✳ BERKS AND BUCKS

Uniform: Black coat, red velvet collar (Hunt staff – scarlet coat, blue velvet collar). Evening Dress: Red, blue collar, white facings.

Chairman: (1974) Roger Palmer, Butlers Farm, Beenham, Reading, Berks RG7 5NT. Tel: 0118 9713330.

President: (1996) Ian Balding, Park House, Kingsclere, Newbury RG15 8PZ. Tel: 01635 298274.

Jt Masters: (1974) R J H D Palmer, Butlers Farm, Beenham, Reading Berks RG7 5NT. Tel: 0118 971 3330; (1991) N Quesnel, Sapphire Cottage, Adwell Farm, Postcombe, Oxon OX9 7DT. Tel: 01844 281021; (1996) D Williams, Hillside Stud, Great Shefford, Hungerford, Berks RG17 7DL. Tel: 01488 638636; (1996) R Cook, Suffield Farm, Suffield Lane. Puttenham, Guildford, Surrey GU3 1BD. Tel: 01483 810220; (1998) M Scholl, Slade Farm, Bucklebury Slade, Reading RG7 6TE. Tel: 01635 868607; (1998) D Fleming, The Old Power House, Marlston, Hermitage, Newbury RG18 9UL. Tel: 01638 200648.

Hon Sec: (1993) D Hawkins, Inversnaid, Chalfont Lane, Chorleywood, Herts WD3 5PP. Tel: 01923 282458.

Point-to-Point Sec: (1993) N Quesnel, Jt Master.

Supporters Club Sec: (1997) Ms Iris Williams, 39 St Michaels Close, Lambourn, Hungerford RG17 8FA. Tel: 01488 73056.

Huntsmen: (1998) Mr R May; Mr D Williams.

KH: (1996) David Gaylard.

Whippers-in: (1998) Mr D Patten, Mr I Smeeth, Miss L Marsh, 25 couple of black and tan Draghounds, the property of Mr & Mrs R J H D Palmer.

Kennels: Hunt Kennels Farm, Baydon Road, Lambourn Woodlands, Hungerford, Berks RG17 7TT. Tel: 01488 71432.

Meet: Sunday and Wednesday.

Subscription: Single £350, family £700, student £240, junior £125. Visitors cap: £50 Adult (£40 Wednesday), Student £20 & £25. Early season £20 for

everyone. Anyone is welcome provided they ring the Hon Sec beforehand.
Lines are arranged by courtesy of the local foxhounds in Berkshire, Buckinghamshire, Hampshire, Oxfordshire and Wiltshire. The area is easily accessible from the M3 and M4 motorways. Each day's lines usually consist of an average nine miles and 50 jumps over at least 95% grassland. Some lines have 90 jumps. Most have easier alternatives where there are big hedges or ditches. Best centres: Newbury, Hungerford, Reading and High Wycombe.

The Hunt was founded in 1974 by Roger Palmer, who still owns the hounds, in order to complement the Palmer Milburn Beagles. Particular emphasis has been placed on hound breeding and building inviting jumps. A special feature is the provision of easier, alternative fences.

Former Masters: N J Henderson, 1974–75. Miss T M Whitworth, 1976–79, Mrs R J H D Palmer, 1979–83. R A Dibley, 1980–86. J Hobby, 1986–88. C J Holmes, 1983–91. W Aeberhard, 1988–91. Mrs S Ensor, 1990–93. I A Balding, 1977–96. H McCall, 1993–96. J Hobby, 1991–98. R Powell, 1995–98.

* BROMYARD

This Pack has now disbanded.

* CAMBRIDGE UNIVERSITY

Uniform: Green, white collar. Evening Dress: Master and Whippers-in may wear Cambridge United Hunt Club coat – Green, white facings, dark blue collar, buff waistcoat.

Jt Masters: (1998) Miss Jennifer Harbison, Newnham College, Cambridge. Tel: 0410 203394; (1998) Miss Jane Walker, Sidney Sussex College, Cambridge. Tel: 01223 523158.

Hon Sec: (1998) Mrs Jenny Ratcliffe, Manor Farm Stud, Chippenham, Cambs. Tel: 01638 720036.

Point-to-Point Sec: (1990) Catherine Scott, 1 Main Street, Wardy Hill, Ely, Cambridgeshire. Tel: 01353 777876.

Huntsman: (1998) Mr Stephen Hill.

KH: (1994) Paul Smith. 10 couple of draft foxhounds, the property of the Masters.

Whippers-in: 1st (1993) Mr Stephen Hill: 2nd (1987) Mr John Dyer.
Kennels: Barton Road, Cambridge. Tel: 01233 262362.
Meet: Sundays, plus occasional bye days.
Subscription: Full £200. Cap: £25; Pony Club/students £10.

The country is hunted by invitation over the country of the Belvoir, Cambridgeshire, Puckeridge, East Sussex, Grafton, Fitzwilliam, Fernie, Quorn, West Norfolk and Woodland Pytchley. The lines are up to about 10 miles long, with one, or sometimes two 'checks'. Obstacles vary according to where the Meet is held, but include hedges, timber and ditches.

The Drag dates back to 1855 with kennels at Cherry Hinton. It was in existence until 1938 and was restarted in 1946 by N E C Sherwood. Thanks to an appeal by Lady Dorothy Bruntisfield, sufficient funds were collected to build new kennels. The present pack is the property of the Masters. No guarantee.

Former Masters: A H Bellingham, 1948–50. M R Kimball, 1948–51. J S Bellingham, 1951–52. E N MacDermott, 1951–52. The Hon D Nall Cain. 1952–53. R T Whiteley, 1952–54. E R de Rothschild, 1953–55. A Lillingston, 1954–56. J Barlow, 1955–56. W Henson, 1956–57. D Rawson-Mackenzie, 1956–58. W Aldous, 1957–59. C S Hall, 1958–59. N Ansell, 1959–60. G Hartigan 1959–60. M C Alhusen, 1960–61. P D Nicholson, 1960–61. J Courtauld, 1960–61. A R P Carden, 1961–62. A F Pemberton, 1961–62. Viscount Ullswater, 1961–63. P A Hill-Walker, 1962–63. Lord Courtenay, 1963–64. P J Scott-Plummer, 1964–65. V Lenox-Conyngham, 1964–65. P J Adams, 1965–66. B G E Munro-Wilson, 1965–67. H W Davies, 1966–67. R A C Drew, 1967–68. C H Gregson, 1966–69. A N Lyndon-Skeggs, 1968–70. A J B Mildmay-White, 1969–70. J P Williams, 1970–71. M Haddon, 1970–71. R Boggis-Rolfe, 1971–72. The Hon S Evans-Freke, 1972–73. R Gilchrist, 1972–73. N Stewart Richardson, 1975–77. W G Lamarque, 1975–77. H C Bellingham, 1975–77. J A Scruby, 1977–78. A C F Tebbutt, 1977–79. James Hurst, 1979–80. P Marshall, 1981–82. J Gorst, 1981–82. The Hon Miss A Elton, 1982–83. The Hon J Henderson, 1982–83. Lt C J Reynolds, 1982–83. W J B Smellie, 1983–84. J Smythe-Osbourne, 1984–86. W Sporborg, 1984–86. G M Johnston, 1986–87. J Black, 1986–87. Miss Sarah Snow, 1987–88. Paul Thomason, 1988–89. Mrs Catherine Scott, 1987–90. Polly Martin, 1989–91. Miss K Church, 1988–92. R J Lee, 1991–92. C Denny,

1991–93. G Pooly, 1992–93. Miss Joanna Holmes, 1992–94. Miss Clare Botterill, 1993–95. Miss Celia Davenort, 1993–96. Miss Arabella Ahern, 1994–96. William Cursham, 1995–1997.

* CELTIC DRAGHOUNDS

Uniform: Peony coat with Royal blue collar and Royal blue facings. Evening dress: Peony.

Jt Masters: (1996) Mrs Geraldine O'Neill; (1997) David Thomas James, Pantygifiela Farm, Bonymaen, Swansea; (1997) Clive Jeffreys Rees, LIB, 18 Walter Road, Swansea. Tel: 01792 470707.

Jt Hon Secs: (1997) Clive Jeffreys Rees. Jt Master; Mrs Diane James, Pantygifiela Farm, Bonymaen, Swansea.

Huntsman: (1997) Mr C J Rees, Jt Master.

KH: (1997) Mr D H Bourne. 15 couple of English/Welsh hounds. Property of the Masters.

Whipper-in: (1997) Mr R J Manning-Rees.

Kennels: Pantygifiela Farm, Bonymaen, Swansea.

Meet: Saturdays and bye days.

Subscription: £150 individual, £200 couple. Cap: £5. Field money: £10.

The country runs from the Vale of Neath in the East to Carmarthen in the West and from Swansea Bay in the South to Builth Wells in the North.

Hunt history: The Celtic Drag hounds was formed at the beginning of 1997 and obtained full registration on the 1st of May 1997. The pack is run on an amateur basis. Drag hunting is a relatively new sport in this part of the world, the only other pack in south Wales being the Llynfi Vale Drag hounds based in Bridgend (qv).

* CHESHIRE FARMERS

Distinctive collar: Evening Dress with cream collar. Black coat with cream collar.

Jt Masters: Snr (1993) J H Harvey, Mill Farm, Mottram St Andrew, Nr Macclesfield Woodford, Cheshire SK7 1RQ; (1994) T F Breen, 12 Northcote Road, Bramhall SK2 2HJ. Tel: 0161 439 5599.

Field Master: Mr S Hague, Jt Master.

Hon Sec: (1994) T F Breen, Jt Master.

Supporters Club Chairperson: Mrs A Harvey.
Point-to-Point Sec: Mrs A E Astall
Huntsman: Mr J Thompson. 20 couple of hounds.
Whipper-in: (1996) Mr D Harvey.
Kennels: Mill Lodge Farm, Mill Lane, Mottram St Andrew SK10 4LW.
Meet: Saturday and occasional bye days.
Subscription: £250. Cap: Subscribers £15, Non-subscribers £40.
The country is a wide variety of terrain from open hill with stone walls to good lowland pasture and arable with hedges and ditches with timber prepared fences when required.
The pack is privately owned and run by the Senior Master, J H Harvey, and was formed by him in 1993 with the assistance of the other now Associate Masters.
Former Masters: B Pickering, 1994–96. J C Dunning, 1993–96.

* THE NORTH EAST CHESHIRE (formerly the Cheshire)

Uniform: Black coat. Committee have red collars; whips have yellow collars. Evening Dress: Black tails with collars as above.
Chairman: (1996) Mr Stephen Ledger, 55 Porchfield Square, Manchester M3 4FG. Tel: 0161 832 1803.
Master: (1993) J Murphy, 116 East Lancs Road, Lowton, Cheshire WA3 1LE. Tel: 01942 671656.
Hon Sec: (1996) Mrs Karen Mellor, Birches Farm, Werneth Low, Gee Cross, Hyde, Cheshire SK14 3AD. Tel: 0161 368 5180.
Supporters Club Sec: (1998) Miss Sarah Johnson, Chatterton End Farm, Mellor, Stockport, Cheshire SK6 5LS. Tel: 0161 427 4713.
KH: (1984) Trevor Tidy (prof). 26 couple of hounds, the property of the hunt.
Whippers-in: (1997) Mr Gary McCafferty, Mr Paul Roberts.
Kennels: Woodseats Lane, Charlesworth, Glossop, Derbyshire. Tel: 01457 853453.
Meet: Saturday, 1 pm.
Subscription: £285 single, £425 family, £30 non-riding, junior £145. Cap: £10, visitors £40.
The country is flat open pasture with hedges and post and rail fences and part moorland with stone walls. Part of the country hunted is that of the

Cheshire Forest Hunt and the Holcombe Harriers. Good centres: The Kilton, High Leigh; The Deanwater, Woodford.

The Hunt was founded in 1958 by Dr G E Burrows with hounds from the High Peak Harriers.

Former Masters: Dr G E Burrows, 1958–65. P Rourke, 1964–68. P E Foster, 1965–68. A committee, 1968–69. Mrs B Meadowcroft, 1969–71. D G Woodward, 1971–72. J P Beaumont, 1972–80. B Powell, 1972–85. M S Ledger, 1984–93. W Tough, 1993–95.

* ISLE OF MAN BLOODHOUNDS DRAG HUNT

Uniform: Pale Yellow, Manx Tartan Blue collar.

Chairman: (1988) Peter Dale, Kerrow-ny-Glough, Greeba, Isle of Man IM4 2DY. Tel: 01624 801515.

Jt Masters: (1974) W A Gilbey, Ballacallin Mooar, Crosby, Isle of Man IM4 2HD. Tel: 01624 851450; (1990) Rev R Harper, Ballawhowin House, St Marks, Isle of Man IM9 3As. Tel: 01624 851251.

Hon Sec: (1991) W A Gilbey, Jt Master.

Huntsman: (1997) Mr J Keeling, 3½ couple of bloodhounds, the property of the Masters.

Whipper-in: (1997) Miss Jayne Ancliffe.

Kennels: Ballahowin, St Marks, Isle of Man. Tel: 01624 851251.

Meet: Saturday, October to March, Boxing Day, New Year's Day.

Cap: Adults £16, juniors £11.

The country covers the whole of the Isle of Man, 32 miles by 12 miles, with its varied countryside. Some of it is low lying and some is hilly. In most areas there are magnificent views across the Island to the sea, often as far as Ireland and England. All the jumps are marked and none is more than 3' 6" high. Many are natural banks and stone walls, but there are also timbered jumps which the Hunt has built in many places.

The Hunt was formed in 1974 by a Committee comprising leading members of the Manx equestrian world. The first Master was Walter Gilbey who had previously been Chairman and co-founder of the Windsor Forest Bloodhounds. Chairman was Jack Kirkpatrick; Mrs Wendy Kirkpatrick was Secretary. Hounds were drafted in from the Windsor Forest by Major Bill Stringer who greatly helped set up the Hunt. Initially, hounds hunted the clean boot, but changed to drag. Always run by a Committee, the Masters make up the shortfall in running costs not met by fees and fund raising. The Isle of Man has a population of just 72,000 and the average field is around 17, although Boxing Day and New Year's day see fields of up to 40. There is no other hunting of any kind on the Island.

Former Masters: B Swain, 1979–80. Mrs D Parkes, 1979–87 Mrs J D W Kirkpatrick, 1981–90. R A Padmore, 1987–94.

* JERSEY

Uniform: Black coat, green collar, distinctive silver button. Hunt Staff: Green coat, black collar.

Jt Masters: (1962) J S O Arthur, Hatherleigh St Mary, Jersey. Tel: 01534 481385; (1997) Mr David Picot, Le Chatelet, Trinity, Jersey. Tel: 01534 863208.

Hon Sec: (1996) Mrs C Campbell, Rockmount, La Rue de la Vallee, St Mary, Jersey JE3 3DL. Tel: 01534 482853.

Hon Treasurer: (1985) I N Ozanne, Les Ruettes Farm, Grands Vaux, St Saviour, Jersey JE2 7HG. Tel: 01534 24721.

KH: (1994) R M Evans.

Whippers-in: (1963) Mr J Phillips; (1994) Mr J F Pryce; (1997) Mr N J S Arthur, 12 couple of harriers, the property of the Committee.

Kennels: Hatherleigh St Mary, Jersey. Tel: 01534 481385.

Meet: Thursday and Saturday.

Subscription: £110. Cap: £15. Attendance limited to members only. Visitors only by permission of the Master.

Drag lines consist of some 8 miles over small fields with banks, hedges and hunt jumps. The season extends from October to March.

The Hunt was formed by officers of British Garrison Battalions stationed in Jersey in the late 19th century, and apart from the two world wars has been in continuous existence since then.

Former Masters: Lt-Col & Mrs C Riley, 1930–39. Major Huelin, 1945. C Biles, 1952–63 M Pitcher, 1946–52 and 1962–71. Major J R C Riley, 1962–98 (died in office).

* LLYNFI VALE

Distinctive collar: Black. Evening Dress: red with black facings. Hunt buttons.

Jt Masters: (1995) Dr D Hamilton Wallis, Bryawel, Glyn Street, Ogmore Vale, Mid Glamorgan CF32 7AS. Tel: 01656 841848; (1995) Mr J Hamilton Wallis, Rhiw Glyn, Bridgend, Mid Glamorgan CF32 7AR. Tel: 01656 841848.

Jt Field Masters: (1995) Mrs Trudy Richards. Tel: 01656 739886; Asst Mr David Richards. Tel: 01656 739886.

Hon Sec: (1995) Mr D Hamilton Wallis, Jt Master.

Point-to-Point Sec: (1998) Mrs Jane Groves, Cwrt Newydd Farm, Bonvilston. Tel: 01446 781179.

Supporters Club Sec: (1998) Mr Sean Daly, Nantmyrth Farm, Shwt Bettws, Bridgend, Mid Glamorgan. Tel: 01656 721378.

Huntsman: (1995) Mr J Hamilton Wallis, Jt Master. Tel: 0976 422215.

KH: (1998) Mr Glyn Ile. 12 couple of Welsh Hounds, the property of the Masters.

Whipper-in: (1997) Mr Nicky Harris.

Kennels: The Old Welsh Water Site, Shwt Road, Shwt, Bettws, Bridgend, Mid Glam.

Meet: Sundays 12 noon and occasional Wednesdays.

Subscription: Apply to Hon Sec.

The country is substantial and diverse including Abergavenny in the north east, the hilly areas from Merthyr Tydfil in the north and Neath in the west and Newport in the east, giving a full range of lowland, forestry plantations, flat grassland and open mountain. Good centres Cowbridge, Llangeinor.

Drag lines consist of some eight miles over diverse terrain negotiating hedges, stone walls and hunt jumps. Lines arranged courtesy of local farmers.

The Pack is privately owned and was established in 1995 by the Jt Masters, D & J Hamilton Wallis. It is the first recognised draghound pack in South Wales, and comprises 12 couple of foxhounds (property of the Masters), drafted from packs around the country.

* NORTH WEST DRAG HUNT

Master: Paul Fletcher, Moss Gate Farm, High Crompton, Shaw, Oldham OL2 7PT. Tel: 01706 846179.

Hon Sec: Mrs Susan Fletcher, as Master.

Huntsman: Mr Paul Fletcher, Master.

Whipper-in: Mrs Janet Boyden.

Meet: Sunday.

Subscription: £20 seniors, £10 under sixteens, no membership as private pack.

The country is from Manchester to the Wirral, up to Garstang and across to Huddersfield, by permission of local landowners and farmers.

* OXFORD DRAGHOUNDS

Uniform: Black coat, Light blue collar. Evening dress: Dark blue.

Hon Master: (1997) Lord Oaksey, Hill Farm, Oaksey, Malmesbury, Wilts.

Jt Masters: (1987) Mr Ashley L Brodin, Lodge Farm, Rossway, Nr Berkhampstead, Herts HP4 3UD; (1992) Mr Greg Parsons, Upperwood Farm Stud, Gaddesden Row, Hertfordshire HP2 6HQ. Tel: 01442 253479; (1996) Mr David Skinner, Kempsons Bungalow, Church Headlands, Whitchurch, Nr Aylesbury, Bucks. Tel: 01296 641162.

Hon Sec: (1990) A L Brodin, c/o Ashley Wilde, Emanuel House, Travellers Lane, Welham Green, Herts AL9 7LD. Tel: 01707 635201.

Huntsman: (1996) Mr David Skinner, Jt Master.

KH: (1992) P Martin (Bicester with Whaddon Chase).

Whipper-in: (1992) Mr Greg Parsons, Jt Master. 7½ couple of foxhounds, the property of the Bicester with Whaddon Chase Hunt.

Kennels: Stratton Audley, Bicester, Oxon. Tel: 01869 277209.

Meet: Sunday, 1.30 pm, November–March.

Subscription: £250. Visitors' cap £35. Visitors welcome.

The country, which lies north, east and south of Oxford, is hunted by kind permission of the Bicester with Whaddon Chase, Grafton and Heythrop and of the farmers of these countries. Occasional meets are also held further afield. The lines are mostly grass, with a great deal of jumping over every type of obstacle. A fast, bold horse with plenty of stamina is required. Best centres are Bicester and Oxford.

The Hunt was formed in 1985 by the amalgamation of the Oxford

University Draghounds and a group of long-standing supporters, to provide a permanent administration. Records of the Oxford University Draghounds can be traced as far back as the first part of the 19th century and the association with the university remains a strong one, with students hunting free in term time and hounds hunted by the student Joint Master.

Former Masters: For pre-1984 see *Baily's* 1985–86 edition. S Miesgaes, 1984–86. R Astley, 1984–86. A C Kyson, 1985–87. Jane Vowles, 1985–88. R McCarthy, 1986–88. Tamsin Browne, 1987–88. R S Colman, 1985–92. D Rose, 1992–94. Miss P Ricketts, 1985–96.

✻ SADDLEWORTH

Uniform: Red coat with green collar. Evening dress: Red.
Chairman: (1988) Brian Powell, Sherbrook Hall Farm, High Stile Lane, Dobcross, Oldham, Lancs. Tel: 01457 873362.
Jt Masters: (1985) B Powell, as above: (1993) Mrs K Clegg, Rakewood, Hollingworth Lake, Littleborough, Lancs. Tel: 01706 378342; (1997) John Bullen, Clarkes Farm, Uppermill, Lancs. Tel: 01457 874795.
Hon Sec: (1993) Rosemary Hamer, 3 Brownlow Avenue, Heyside, Oldham, Lancs. Tel: 01706 840245.
Point-to-Point Sec: Corrina Hirst, Moorhouse Farm, Reynolds Lane, Betchton Heath, Sandbach, Cheshire. Tel: 0127 759439.
Huntsman: Mr B Powell, Jt Master.
KH: (1988) Peter Carter.
Whipper-in: (1985) Neil Bailey, 6 couple of foxhounds, the property of Mr B Powell.
Kennels: Sherbrook Hall Farm, High Stile Lane, Dobcross. Tel: 01457 873362.
Meet: Saturday.
Subscription: £200. Cap £25.
The country is located on the west side of the Pennines to the north of Stalybridge (Manchester) and south of Todmorden, skirting Saddleworth Moor. It is very varied terrain but predominantly hilly, long lay grass, with stone walls. Adjacent hunts: Rockwood Harriers, North East Cheshire Drag Hunt, Holcombe Harriers.
The Hunt was re-established in 1985, after a break of 100 years, under the

Chairman, B Powell MDH. Jt Master of the North East Cheshire Drag Hunt for 14 years.

* WEST SHROPSHIRE

Distinctive Collar: Wedgwood blue.

Jt Masters: (1981) John S Lee, Fron Llwyd, Welshpool, Powys. Tel: 01938 553230; (1991) Harold Pugh, Grove Farm, Kinton, Shropshire. Tel: 01743 741338; (1984) Jonathan A Lee, Keepers Cottage, Hope Road, Leighton, Welshpool, Powys. Tel: 01938 552238; (1998) Philip Jones, Pant Farm, Guilsfield, Powys. Tel: 01938 850300.

Hon Sec: (1990) John S Lee, as above.

Huntsman: (1997) Mr J A Lee, Jt Master. 6 couple of English hounds, the property of John S Lee.

Kennels: Trawscoed Hen, Guilsfield.

Meet: Saturday with occasional bye day Thursday.

Subscription: Apply to Hon Sec.

The country is good natural land, with hedges, post and rails, etc. Best centres: Pentre and Knockin.

The pack, privately owned and run by John S Lee, was formed by him when the West Shropshire Foxhounds, of which he had been one of the Joint Masters for over ten years, was discontinued after the 1980–81 season.

Former Masters: A Birchall, 1986–91. J S Lee, 1981–95. John W R Evans, 1986–97. Alan Birchall, 1995–97.

* STAFF COLLEGE AND ROYAL MILITARY ACADEMY SANDHURST

Uniform: Black with green collar (Hunt staff).

Jt Masters: (1987) Miss P Sutton, Barleywood Farm, West Worldham, Alton, Hants; (1995) Capt Tim Hymes, RMAS Camberley, Surrey; (1997) A Vanoostrum, Fording, New Mill, Eversley, Hants RG27 0RA. Tel: 01252 614788; (1997) Wing Cdr Nick Hudson, RMAS Camberley, Surrey.

Field Master: Andrew Vanoostrum.

Hon Sec: (1992) Brian Stern, Stable Cottage, Wheatsheaf Road, Henfield, West Sussex BN5 9AU. Tel: 01273 494482 or 495188 (day).

Point-to-Point Sec: Ms C Elliott, Craft Stables, Paice Lane, Medstead, Alton, Hants GU34 5PT. Tel: 01420 562268.

Supporters Club Sec: (1994) M Mitchell, 43 Addiscombe Road, Crowthorne, Berkshire. Tel: 01344 772528.

Huntsman: (1975) Miss P Sutton, Jt Master.

Kennelman: (1997) Bryan Robinson.

Whipper-in: (1994) Mr Jonathan Cook. 8 couple of hounds.

Kennels: RMAS, Camberley, Surrey. Tel: 01276 63344, ext 2405.

Meet: Wednesday and occasionally Sunday.

Subscription: £250. Cap £30.

The country is bounded in the north by Waltham St Lawrence, in the east by Tweseldown, in the south by Rotherfield, and in the west by Preston Candover.

A private pack, it was established in 1870, and maintained by Officers of the Staff College and Officers and Officer Cadets of the RMA, Sandhurst. The pack was put down in 1939 and restarted in 1947 by Lt-Col M J Lindsay, DSO, KDG, a student at the 1947 Staff College course. In 1963 the Hunt divided into two packs, and the Sandhurst & Bisley Foxhounds became a separate civilian Hunt; the Drag continued under its present name.

Former Masters: Capt Hon H Legge, Coldstream Guards, 1870–71. For Masters from 1871 to 1950, see *Baily's* 1937–38 and later editions. Major J R Cleghorn, DSO, 1951–52. Maj-Gen G Dawnay, DSO, 1951–54. Capt W S P Lithgow, RA, 1951–54. Capt R P M Spencer, KDG, 1952–54. Major P H V de O'Grady, RA, 1954–56. Capt M J M Thomas, Life Guards, 1954–56. Major C H F Coaker, RHA, Major J Clarke Kennedy, MC, 12th Lancers, 1956–57. M S Close, 1956–57. Major R S Ferguson. MVO, RNF 1957–59. Major P J Holland, MC, 16/5 Lancers, 1957–60. Lt-Col J M Strawson, QRIH, 1960–61. Brig C H Blacker, OBE, MC, Lt-Col J R C Riley, Coldstream Guards, 1961–62. Capt T W Kopanski, RA, 1961–62. Major J L S Andrews, RA, 1962–64. Capt J R T Phipps, RA, 1962–64. Maj-Gen H J Mogg, 1964–65. Major P Bengough, 1964–65. Lt-Col W S P Lithgow, RA, 1965–67. Capt P Wainwright, RWF, 1965–67. Major J D Archer, Inniskillings, 1966–68. Lt-Col M R Johnston, QDG, 1966–68. Lt-Col A W Dennis, 16/5L, 1968–69. Capt C Turner, 4/7 D G, 1968–69. Lt-Col P M Hamer, OBE, 11H, 1968–69. Capt P C E Fishbourne, Scots DG, 1970–72. Lt-Col A R Douglas-Nugent, 17/21L, 1970–73. Major P J

Marzetti, RCT, 1973–74. Capt E C W Morrison, 5 Innis DG, 1972–74. Lt-Col R H G McCarthy, 15/19H. 1974–75. Capt W I Hurrell, 17/21L, 1974–75. Capt L M Borwick, Scots DG, 1974–76. Lt-Col R H Swinburn, 17/21L, 1975–77. Capt M T Ward, 13/18H, 1976–78. Lt-Col R J S Baddeley, 4/7 DG, 1977–78. Capt M R Bromley-Gardener, 1979–80. Lt-Col R J W ffrench Blake, 13/18H, 1979–81. Capt M H K Green, 13/18H, 1980–82. Lt-Col J R Smales, 14/20H, 1981–84. Capt H L A Macdonald, QDG, 1982–84. Lt-Col V A L Goodhew, 1984–85. Capt C Coldrey, 1984–85. Lt-Col C K Price, 1984–86. Lt-Col A A J R Cummings, 17/21L, 1986–88. Capt T F S Hall Wilson, Scots DG, 1986–88. Major D H O de Stacpoole, IG, 1987–88. Lt-Col J H T Short, 9/12L, 1988–89. Lt-Col S J M Jenkins, 4/7 DG, 1988–90. Lt-Col A P de Ritter, LG, 1989–90. Major M R Lilley, RCT, 1990–91. Capt H Bucknell, CG, 1992–93. Lt Col Hamish MacDonald, GDG, 1992–94. Maj David Foster, IG, 1992–93. Capt Dominic Mahony, LG, 1992–94. Lt Col John Deverell, 1994–95. Capt Charles Whittaker, 1994–95. C Hill, 1992–96. Col Chris Day, 1995–96.

* MID-SURREY FARMERS

Uniform: Dark blue coat (Whippers-in and markers), dark green coats with Hunt buttons (members).

Chairman: (1996) The Hon Mr Justice Cazalet, Shaws Farm, Plumpton Green, Nr Lewes, Sussex.

Jt Masters: (1976) Douglas Bunn, Hickstead Place, Hickstead, Sussex. Tel: 01273 834666; (1978) Mrs P M Marshall, Stone Cottage, Broadstone Warren, Forest Row, E Sussex. Tel: 01342 822315; (1981) David Robinson, Northease Farm, Rodmell, Lewes, Sussex. Tel: 01273 474983; (1991) Peter Webb, 6 Lewes Crescent, Brighton, BN2 1FH. Tel: 01273 671846; (1994) George Goring, Goring Hotel, Beeston Place, Grosvenor Gardens, London W1. Tel: 0171-396 9000.

Hon Sec: (1978) Mrs P M Marshall, Jt Master.

Point-to-Point Sec: (1978) Mrs D Donegan, Chart Stud Farm, Heaverham, Sevenoaks, Kent. Tel: 01732 61451.

Huntsman: (1998) Mr Fred French.

KH: Mark Bycroft, Old Surrey & Burstow.

Whipper-in: (1984) Colin Baker. 8 couple of hounds, the property of the Hunt.

Kennels: c/o The Old Surrey & Burstow Foxhounds, Felbridge, W Sussex.
Meet: Saturday, 1–1.30 pm.
Subscription: £375 single, £475 double. Cap: £10.
Meets are held in the Old Surrey & Burstow, West Kent, Southdown & Bridge, Crawley & Horsham, Chiddingfold, Leconfield & Cowdray, and East Sussex & Romney Marsh countries by kind permission of the Masters of these packs.
This pack originated some 60 years ago as the Banstead Drag, then changed to Mid-Surrey Drag. It was disbanded as the outbreak of war, revived in the season 1947–48, and is now know as Mid-Surrey Farmers' Drag Hounds. Attendance is limited to members only; visitors only by permission of the Master.
Former Masters: Major E Howard, 1926–47, Hon P Kindersley, 1947–87. Sir Edward Cazalet, 1973–97.

TRENT VALLEY (THE FARRIERS HARRIERS)

Uniform: Forest green coat with forest green collar.
Master: (1991) Philip Humphrey, Forge Farm, Moor Lane, Gotham, Notts NG11 0LH. Tel: 0115 983 1117.
Jt Hon Secs: (1993) Mrs Jane Bradwell, Wolds Farm, Fosse Way, Cotgrave, Notts NG12 3GH. Tel: 0115 989 9717; (1993) Mrs André Wilson, North Lodge Bungalow, Widmerpool, Notts. Tel: 0115 937 5450.
Huntsman: (1991) Mr P Humphrey, Master.
Whippers-in: (1991) Mr E Kopel; Mr T Arris; Mr M Humphrey.
Kennels: Forge Farm, Moor Lane, Gotham, Notts. Tel: 0115 983 1117.
Meet: Sunday, 2 pm.
The country is some 18 miles east to west by 40 miles north to south. The north east is mainly arable with hunt jumps; the south west is mainly grass with a variety of hedges, rails and ditches. Wire is usually removed. Drag lines are arranged by courtesy of local farmers and foxhound packs in Leicestershire and Nottinghamshire, and are on average 8–10 miles.
The pack was established in 1991 and is privately owned by the Master. The hounds were drafted from Harrier packs and comprise 10 couple.

Ireland

COMERAGH MOUNTAIN DRAGHOUNDS
Uniform: Coat, black or blue (Ladies), Red collar, Hunt Staff: Green coat, red collar.
Jt Masters: (1997) Mr Clive Holmes & Mrs Suzanne Holmes, Comeragh House, Kilmacthomas, Co Waterford. Tel: 051 291359.
Hon Sec: (1997) Mrs Suzanne Holmes, Jt Master.
Huntsman: (1997) J Keane.
Whipper-in: (1997) D Nolan. 9 couple bloodhounds, the property of the Jt Masters.
Kennels: Mayfield, Portlaw, Co Waterford. Tel: 051 387503.
Meet: Sunday.
Subscription: None.
The country is across Co Waterford from the Comeragh Mountains to the sea and north to the Kilkenny border. Mainly open country and grassland with formidable Irish banks, drains, stone walls and incorporating man made 'natural' fly fences. Needs a bold, brave and careful horse with stamina and speed. Share country with the numerous foxhunting and harrier packs.
The Hunt is the only drag hunt in S E Ireland and was formed in 1997 as a private pack with hunting by invitation only.

Select Bibliography

Baily's Hunting Directory, 1998-1999 Edition

Beckford, Peter, *Thoughts on Hunting*, 3rd Edition, London, 1912

B.B. (Denys Watkins-Pitchford), *Wild Lone*, 1970 Edition, London

Blackwood, William, *Tales of the Horse*, 1969, Edinburgh and London

Coaten, Arthur W. (Ed.), *British Hunting*

Dickens, Charles, *David Copperfield*

Hastings, Max, *Outside Days*, Revised Edition, London, 1995

Hunt Diaries and other Records of the Royal Artillery (Woolwich) Drag and (Bordon) Drag

Hunt Diaries and other Records of the Staff College Drag

Journals of The Household Brigade

Sassoon, Siegfried, *Memoirs of a Fox-Hunting Man*, London, 1954 Edition

Scruton, Roger, *On Hunting*, London, 1998

Somerville, William, *The Chase*

Somerville & Ross, *Put Down One and Carry Two*

Surtees, Robert Smith, *Handley Cross, Mr Sponge's Sporting Tour*

The Times, December 6 1997, Article on Drag-Hunting by Lin Jenkins

Trevelyan, G.M., *English Social History*, London Edition, 1946

Trollope, Anthony, *The Claverings, The Kellys and the O'Kellys, Phineas Finn, Phineas Redux, Mr Scarborough's Family*

Williams, Dorian, *The Horse in Literature*

Index